# MIRACLE MOMENTS
## IN
# MICHIGAN WOLVERINES
## FOOTBALL HISTORY
### BEST PLAYS, GAMES, AND RECORDS

**Derek Kornacki and Steve Kornacki**
**Foreword by Glenn E. "Shemy" Schembechler III**

**SPORTS PUBLISHING**

Sports Publishing books may be purchased in bulk at special discounts for sales promotion, corporate gifts, fund-raising, or educational purposes. Special editions can also be created to specifications. For details, contact the Special Sales Department, Sports Publishing, 307 West 36th Street, 11th Floor, New York, NY 10018 or sportspubbooks@skyhorsepublishing.com.

Sports Publishing® is a registered trademark of Skyhorse Publishing, Inc.®, a Delaware corporation.

Visit our website at www.sportspubbooks.com.

10 9 8 7 6 5 4 3 2 1

Library of Congress Cataloging-in-Publication Data is available on file.

Cover design by Tom Lau

Cover photo credit: Associated Press

ISBN: 978-1-68358-191-8

Ebook ISBN: 978-1-68358-192-5

Printed in China

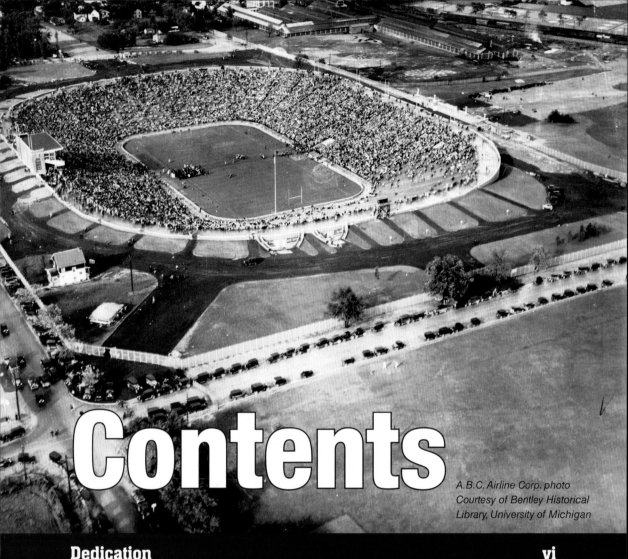

# Contents

*A.B.C. Airline Corp. photo*
*Courtesy of Bentley Historical*
*Library, University of Michigan*

# Part Two: Crisler and the Modern Era

# Part Three: "THE TEAM! THE TEAM! THE TEAM!"

# Part Four: The Tradition Continues

For Scarlett, Mary, Cheyne, and Brad. For everyone I've had the pleasure of sharing a football Saturday with, and for all the "cotton-pickin' maize-and-blue hearts" across the world and across time.

# Introduction

In the summer of 1989 I was eight years old, and my father, Steve, who was covering Michigan football for the *Detroit Free Press* at the time, took me and my younger brother, Brad, to the offices of the athletic department on State Street in Ann Arbor. He was there to talk to Bo Schembechler for a story he was working on that day, and he sat us down in the sweltering lobby of the building and gave me a dollar to buy candy from the vending machine while we waited. Brad and I went over to the vending machine and grabbed two packages of Reese's Peanut Butter Cups. The only problem was that they'd been baking in that sauna of a lobby for who knows how long and were completely melted. But when has that ever stopped a kid from eating chocolate? Just as I'm shoving the last clump of melted chocolate goo into my mouth, the door swings open, and standing in the doorway is Bo. And in his Bo voice, he shouts out, "Come on in here, boys, I wanna show you guys something!" Now I'd been to a few games at this point, and I certainly knew who Bo Schembechler was, but I'd never met him before. I'd only seen him from a distance, and I was completely awestruck. As I made my way toward the entrance of his office, it felt like I was being moved there on a conveyor belt. It was the first time in my life that I can remember feeling an overwhelming sense that I was in the presence of greatness. When I got inside his office, he reached out his hand and said, "Hello son, I'm Bo Schembechler, nice to meet you." It was at that moment that I suddenly realized that my hands were completely covered in chocolate. But what was I gonna do... not shake the hand of this great man? So I stuck out the sorriest excuse of a dead-fish handshake, and Bo says, "That's no way to shake a man's hand! You gotta look him in the eye and give him a nice, firm shake!" I'm thirty-six years old now, and I've tried to honor Bo's advice with each handshake I've given since then. We had a blast with him that day. He told us stories and let us hold a bunch of trophies (that we probably got chocolate all over). He asked us what year we were going to graduate from high school and asked if we were going to come play football at Michigan. He was so kind and gracious and really made us feel like we were his friends. It truly was one of the best days of my childhood.

When I think about it, so many of the best days of my life have had Michigan football and Michigan athletics at the center of them. I think back to watching Michigan away games in our living room with my mother, Mary, Brad, and our older brother, Cheyne. We'd jump up and down and scream at the TV. My mom would order pizza at halftime, and afterward, we'd go play pickup football with the other boys in the neighborhood. I remember going to the home games with my brothers and our friends and collecting bottles and cans from the tailgates and cashing them in for money to buy tickets to the game. I recall the whole family going to the '92 Rose Bowl game and saying a prayer at halftime that if Michigan could just win the game, I'd never ask for anything again (Washington beat them, 34–14). I was in Michigan Stadium when Colorado threw the Hail Mary pass in '94, but I was also there to storm the field after the '97 win over Ohio State. Brad and I jumped up and down and hugged and yelled. We slapped the shoulder pads of the players and hugged Michigan fans we didn't even know. Then to witness them hoist the Rose Bowl trophy and win a national championship that same season was an absolutely perfect day.

I had the pleasure of interviewing the longtime voice of Michigan football, Jim Brandstatter, for this book. And when I asked him what the Michigan tradition means to him, he replied, "Oh, wow. To me, it's like a security blanket. When there's trouble in the world, when there are questions and uncertainty, you know there will be a certainty about Michigan football. That it will be solid and good, and the players will be good, and the uniforms won't change, and you're going to be proud of the product they put on the field. That's what the tradition means to me. It means that guys who played all the way back in the heydays of the Tom Harmons and the Willie Hestons and Fielding H. Yosts, if they were transported in time to the stadium and they looked down and watched them run out of the tunnel to play the game, they would all take pride in wearing their letter jackets, standing on the sideline, they'd say, 'I was a part of that.' That's what the Michigan tradition is to me. It's security, a safe haven, and when things are in flux, there's one thing you know you can count on. And it's the winged helmet and Michigan football."

Think of how lucky we all are to be a part of this family, this "TEAM," this "Michigan of ours."

Over the years, the Michigan football program has produced innumerable boyhood heroes and coaches I've deeply admired as an adult. But there's no one I admire more, and no one who's a bigger hero to me, than my father, Steve. Working on this book with him will be something I will cherish forever. I hope that the reader enjoys the stories as much as we've enjoyed telling them. GO BLUE!!

Derek Kornacki

# Foreword

If you want to understand the mark of a great coach regardless of what sport or era in which they coached in, simply ask the players who were fortunate enough to play for them. There are those coaches who were able to achieve both wins and championships without losing their true mission in life. Glenn E. "Bo" Schembechler accomplished that, and so many of those he coached are today doing their very best to pass that on to the next generations. Just ask Dr. William L. Taylor Jr.

Billy Taylor was blessed with a great amount of talent and ability that went far beyond breaking tackles and scoring touchdowns, but when you are a young freshman at the University of Michigan, you can't be sure what you can achieve. Bo Schembechler changed all that when he arrived in Ann Arbor in the winter of 1969 in what began a friendship that was forged in stone until his death in 2006.

Bo demanded more than anyone Taylor had ever seen or been around, and it focused on true accountability out of yourself and your team. He held his players to a standard of behavior that had little forgiveness, and that was forged into greatness. The wins and championships quickly arrived, and true momentum was built in those early days. Those lessons taught what it means to be resilient against all adversity, and there was never really a time that anyone in the program didn't believe in themselves or their teammates.

All that changed for Billy during that fateful season of 1971, when an All-American career came crashing down amidst personal tragedy that would have destroyed most of us—the death of his mother, who was the center of his life, quickly followed by his favorite uncle who murdered his wife and then committed suicide. And as if that wasn't enough, Billy's girlfriend was murdered in Detroit, where all these events happened in just nine short months. An injury-shortened NFL career was the beginning of battles with addiction and depression that spanned years and decades. It led to divorce, homelessness, and even the worst condition of all, loss of hope.

Billy Taylor receives the 1971 Michigan football MVP award from coach Bo Schembechler, his mentor for life, as co-captain Frank Gusich looks on.
*Courtesy of Bentley Historical Library, University of Michigan.*

The prevailing opinion about college coaches is that when a young man signs his letter of intent to go play for a school it is for the next four or five years, and then it is done. That was far from the truth when it came to Bo. The letter of intent in his mind was a lifetime contract that will never end. It was Bo who continued to help and counsel Billy to deliver him from despair to the heights of success, simply because he would never give up on any of his players. He was there when they needed him, anytime, anywhere.

Fittingly, today Dr. Taylor is fulfilling lifetime contracts much like Bo did in the form of his "Get Back Up" program that coaches and counsels those facing the same struggles he did. If you were to ask Billy today if he found his mission in life, he would say "Absolutely!" and a lot of it is because of Coach Bo.

This is only one example of the thousands that are out there today that continue to serve in the same way that their old coach did. And you can be sure that Coach is smiling down from heaven because of it. How do I know this? Just ask them!

Many of Bo's players—Rick Leach, Rob Lytle, Anthony Carter, Jim Harbaugh, and Desmond Howard—are among those featured in *Miracle Moments in Michigan Wolverines Football History*, along with an in-depth look at the 1969 upset of Ohio State and the memorable touchdown pass from John Wangler to A.C. that beat Indiana on the final play in 1979. Longtime Wolverines beat writer Steve Kornacki and his son, Derek, will take you from Fielding H. Yost and the writing of "The Victors" to the present.

Enjoy!

Go Blue! Those Who Stay Will Be Champions!

Glenn E. "Shemy" Schembechler III

*Glenn Edward "Shemy" Schembechler III has been a scout for the Washington Redskins, Kansas City Chiefs, Seattle Seahawks, and Chicago Bears. He also was the assistant recruiting coordinator at the University of Michigan. He has worked with renowned coaches such as Joe Gibbs, Marty Schottenheimer, Gary Moeller, Lloyd Carr, and his father, Michigan Hall of Fame coach Bo Schembechler. Shemy now heads GES Advisory Company, which scouts and works to place high school football recruits with schools from NAIA to Division I. He lives in Columbus, Ohio, with his wife, Megan, and their son, Glenn Edward "Bo" Schembechler IV.*

# PART ONE

## THE BEGINNINGS AND YOST

# Michigan Teaches Notre Dame How to Play Football in 1887

It is more than fitting that the first intercollegiate football game that Notre Dame ever played in its storied history was against the University of Michigan. That 130 years later the only program that has a better win total than the Fighting Irish is the very program that taught them the early rules of the burgeoning sport.

In the fall of 1887, two Michigan students who had previously attended Notre Dame named George W. DeHaven and William W. Harless wrote to their friend and former mentor, Brother Paul (who is credited with founding modern athletics at Notre Dame) and asked if he'd be interested in assembling a team to participate in one or two very informal games. At the time, the sport was more or less an intramural activity at Notre Dame and the rules by which the game was played varied from school to school and region to region. Michigan was considered to be the leading practitioners of the "rugby football" style of the sport in the region at that time, and they offered to teach Brother Paul and his students the rules by which they played the game. Brother Paul accepted, and on the damp, chilly morning of November 23, 1887, the University of Michigan football team arrived in South Bend for the very first time.

According to an account from Arthur J. Hope's book, *Notre Dame: One Hundred Years*, the visiting team, "After spending a few hours taking in the surroundings, donned their uniforms of spotless white and appeared upon the senior campus." The squads were divided into teams of half Michigan players and half Notre Dame players so that the Michigan players could properly teach the rules of the rugby football style to their inexperienced challengers. After a short scrimmage, the Notre Dame players felt like they had the hang of it, and the two teams took to their respective sidelines with their classmates. They played what was then called an "inning," with Michigan coming out on top, 8–0.

The two teams joined together for a postgame lunch at noon, after which the Michigan team was given an extremely warm send-off as they boarded their carriage for the Niles train station, just across the Indiana-Michigan border.

The Michigan football team continued on to Chicago to play a scheduled game the next day, but an indelible impression had been left on the student body at Notre Dame. Days later, the Notre Dame student newspaper, *The Scholastic,* reported that "the game had started an enthusiastic football boom." One that has grown beyond anything anyone in attendance 130 years ago could have even imagined. One that has spawned one of the sport's greatest programs and one of its most enduring, respectful and fierce rivalries.

## Elbel Writes 'The Victors' After Inspirational Win in 1898

It is widely considered that the two most stirring and recognizable fight songs in all of college football are Notre Dame's "The Victory March" and Michigan's "The Victors." And in a long list of similarities and ironies that the two historic programs share is the little-known fact that Louis Elbel, the twenty-one-year-old music student who penned "The Victors," was born and raised in South Bend, Indiana.

Very little is known about what brought Elbel to attend the University of Michigan (other than those reasons that are obvious to anyone who's spent time on the campus and in Ann Arbor), but a good deal is known about what brought him to Chicago, Illinois, on Thanksgiving Day of 1898.

Michigan was to play the legendary coach Amos Alonzo Stagg and his power-house University of Chicago Maroons for the Western Conference (the predecessor of the Big Ten conference) championship.

A crowd of 12,000 spectators gathered that day to take in the game. It's estimated that roughly 1,000 or so of them were Michigan fans who'd traveled by train, Elbel among them. Michigan jumped out to an early lead over the favored Maroons on a Charles Widman touchdown, and the following Neil Snow extra point made the score 6–0. Toward the end of the first half, Chicago kicked a 30-yard field goal (which was worth five points at that time), making the score 6–5 at the half. In the second half, Widman scored his second touchdown of the day. He broke loose on a delayed, lateral pass play (somewhat rare at the time) and rumbled 65 yards for the score. The run sent everyone from Ann Arbor who witnessed it into a frenzy and maintained a cherished place in the memories of all Michigan football fans of the era. When asked to recall the play by the *Chicago Daily Tribune*, Widman stated, "The play was a revolving wedge on Chicago's left tackle. Their end and tackle had been drawn in by our men, and when the ball was given to me on a delayed pass I had a clear field, except for the Chicago backs. I ran as fast as I could diagonally across the field, realizing that I was hotly pursued." Snow added the extra point, making the score 12–5. Michigan was in the driver's seat until Chicago added a late touchdown and extra point of their own, bringing the Maroons to within one point, 12–11. The maize and blue forced Chicago to punt on their final possession, and when Michigan had ticked the final seconds off the clock, they were champions of the Western Conference for the first time in school history.

After the game had ended, the thousand-plus Michigan fans in attendance formed a line behind the student band and paraded through the University of Chicago campus and onto the streets of Chicago, singing songs and cheers well into the night.

Of that night, Elbel would recall years later, "We were crazed with joy. We paraded in the dark. We yelled and followed our UofM band, singing to the tune of 'Hot Time in the Old Town.' It struck me quite suddenly that such an epic should be dignified by something more elevating, for this was no ordinary victory. My spirits were so uplifted that I was clear off the earth, and that is when 'The Victors' was inspired. I put in a lot of 'hails' and I knew the fellows would get them in with the proper emphasis. Through them, the title suggested itself, and I dedicated it to the Michigan team of 1898."

Days after the famous victory over Chicago, Elbel, with a full heart, sat down and wrote these words:

> *"Hail to the victors valiant!*
> *Hail to the conq'ring heroes!*
> *Hail! Hail to Michigan*
> *The leaders and best!*
> *Hail to the victors valiant!*
> *Hail to the conq'ring heroes!*
> *Hail! Hail to Michigan*
> *The champions of the west!"*

"The Victors" was published in early 1899 and first played to the public on April 5 of the same year at an on-campus musical by a student orchestra conducted by Elbel himself. The song received such praise that an encore performance was requested by both students and faculty. Three days later, an orchestra lead by none other than John Philip Sousa (one of the most notable composers of the time) played the song before an audience in Ann Arbor. Sousa would go on to say years later that "The Victors" was "one of the nation's finest military marches and the best original college song" he had ever heard.

The song would also go on to serve as a morale booster in the First World War, being played by both the French and German military bands and serving as the song of the 125th Infantry of Michigan as they marched into captured Germany in 1918.

Elbel himself would go on to Germany (fortunately before WWI broke out) after graduating from Michigan to study classical piano. He later toured with several orchestras in both Europe and the United States. He ultimately decided that after a few years of touring he'd like to go back home to South Bend and work in his family's music store. Right around the time that he would have arrived back in South Bend, there were two brothers by the names of Michael and John Shea who were attending school at Notre Dame. Shortly after finishing their undergraduate degrees in 1904 and 1906, respectively, the brothers traveled to Ann Arbor to see their beloved Notre Dame take on Michigan at Ferry Field in the 1908 matchup. Michigan won the game by a score of 12–6. After hearing "The Victors" played for what had to feel like hundreds of times to them that day, they decided that Notre Dame needed a fight song of its own, and shortly thereafter, the Shea brothers had completed what would come to be known as "The Victory March," further intertwining the school's football traditions and giving the sport its two finest fight songs.

Louis Elbel would spend the rest of his days living and working in South Bend, but he would faithfully return every year for the homecoming game until his death in 1959. He came back to lead the band of young students in the song that he wrote, that was born out of a burning elation and adoration, on a cold night, all those years earlier in Chicago, in his youth.

Louis Elbel leads the Michigan Marching Band in his "The Victors," arguably the top college fight song ever written, at Michigan Stadium in 1955.
*Courtesy of Bentley Historical Library, University of Michigan.*

# The Story Behind the Little Brown Jug

The college football landscape is littered with "rivalry trophies." There are some such as The Golden Boot (Arkansas vs. LSU) and The Stanford Axe (Cal vs. Stanford) that most devout fans of the sport would at least be somewhat familiar with. Then you've got your Milk Can (Boise State vs. Fresno State) and your War on I-4 Trophy (UCF vs. South Florida), which are all well and good. They're trophies manufactured to give some physically tangible meaning to a game. Then there are the ones that happen organically—the ones that make a program and its entire fan base sick to their stomachs if they aren't sitting in their trophy case. And the most enduring and best known of these trophies is, of course, The Little Brown Jug.

The Wolverines had won 29 straight games when they headed to Minnesota in 1903 to take on the 10–0 Golden Gophers in one of the biggest games to be played in the early years of college football. Now I'm not sure if the entire reason for the jug even being purchased speaks more to the suspicious mind of Fielding H. Yost, or if it speaks more to the state of college football at the time, but the story goes that Yost had a team manager buy the jug at a variety store in Minneapolis in fear of the Gophers providing his team with contaminated drinking water for the game. Whatever the reason, the jug was left behind after a 6–6 tie as Michigan rushed to make a train to Chicago. I'm sure that the Wolverines departed Minneapolis angrily after the game being called early on account of the fans rushing the field after Minnesota tied the game with two minutes remaining. The jug was probably the last thing on any Wolverine's mind at that point.

The next morning after the game, the jug was discovered by the Minnesota equipment manager, Oscar Munson. He then brought the jug to the office of the then athletic director, L. J. Cooke. The Minnesota football team was probably more than a little insulted that Yost did not trust them to provide the Michigan team with clean drinking water, so Munson and Cooke decided to give the jug a little makeover. They painted 'Michigan Jug—Captured by Oscar, October 31, 1903' on one side, and then painted 'Minnesota 6—Michigan 6' on the other (making the Minnesota "6" significantly larger). Then they proceeded to have the jug suspended from the ceiling of Cooke's office, where it hung until the teams met again in 1909.

It's not exactly clear what happened when Yost expressed his desire to have the jug returned to Ann Arbor, but the most likely scenario is that Yost's request was met with Cooke telling him that if he wanted it back he'd have to come play them for it. And in 1909, that's just what Yost and his Wolverines did, with Michigan winning the game, 15–6. Yost made damn sure that he didn't leave the jug behind this time, and with the jug back securely in Ann Arbor, the rivalry was born. The Wolverines won again in 1910, and because of Michigan's withdrawal from the Western Conference, the rivalry game was not played again until 1919.

In 1931, the jug was stolen from the Michigan Athletic Administration Building, and two months later a car carrying four goggled men dropped a jug off at an Ann Arbor gas station. The public was skeptical of the jug's authenticity, but Yost claimed it to be the real deal. Two years later, another jug appeared in some bushes next to the medical building on campus, and upon close inspection, Yost deemed this jug to be the original, and it's the one that has been in the possession of either the Michigan or Minnesota equipment manager ever since. However, the Michigan equipment manager is far more familiar with the trophy, seeing as Michigan holds a 55–12 lead in the rivalry series, including 39 of the last 43.

(Left to Right) Michigan athletic director Fielding H. Yost, assistant coach Wally Weber, assistant coach Bennie Oosterbaan, assistant coach Jack Blott, assistant coach Franklin Cappon, and head coach Harry Kipke pose in 1931 with the Little Brown Jug and a copy made of it because the original had disappeared.
*Courtesy of Bentley Historical Library, University of Michigan.*

The rivalry may be tilted heavily in Michigan's favor, but the game and the Little Brown Jug still endure as one of college football's most beloved institutions. It beautifully represents the love of tradition that all college football fans hold so dear. Long may it live.

# Coach Fielding H. Yost

According to legend, sometime between 1897 and 1901, Fielding H. Yost was in Columbus, Ohio, being interviewed by members of a board tasked with finding the next Ohio State head football coach. At some point during the interview, Yost decided to challenge the board members to a push-up contest and as a result is asked to leave the meeting. Now there's no record of this occurring, and there's no one alive who could corroborate the details as they happened. No one really knows who first told the story, but what we do know about Yost, the tale is entirely plausible. In fact, it would not be surprising if the origins reach directly back to Yost himself. He was a brash, intense, high-energy braggart who met every challenge and endeavor with enthusiasm, and when he entered a room, he owned it. He was a cigar-smoking, teetotaling, devout Christian who loved to spin a yarn and loved to be surrounded by people.

Yost was born on April 30, 1871, on a farm in Fairview, West Virginia. The land had been in his family since 1825. His father was a veteran of the Civil War on the Confederate side, and this unfortunately colored certain aspects of his worldview.

After high school, Yost attended Fairmont Normal School in Fairmont, West Virginia, where he studied to be a teacher. After one year at Fairmont, he decided to transfer to Ohio Normal School (now Northern Ohio University) in large part because they offered sports. After receiving his teaching certificate, he decided not to pursue teaching, opting to attend law school instead. In the fall of 1895, Yost enrolled in the law school at West Virginia University. It was there that he would play his college football (it was common for graduate students to compete in athletics in those days because there were no rules on eligibility), and at 6-foot, 200 pounds, was a formidable left tackle.

It's clear that by the time he left law school at West Virginia in 1896, Yost had a very firm grasp on the finer points of the game of football. This was illustrated in his first season as a head coach the following year at Ohio Wesleyan University, where his varsity football team went 7–1–1, tying the University of Michigan and beating Ohio State.

In the early years of organized college football, it was rare that a coach stayed at one school for more than a few years. They were often contracted only one year at a time, and they would show up at the start of the fall semester and leave once it had ended—usually off to a new destination. Their pay was modest, and it was something that most coaches only did for a few years between earning their college degrees and starting careers. So, in keeping in line with the practices of the time, Yost was off to the University of Nebraska for the 1898 season, where his team went 8–3. Then it was one state south for the 1899 season, where his University of Kansas team went 10–0, outscoring opponents 280–37.

In the fall of 1900, Yost arrived in Palo Alto, California, where he led Stanford to a 7–2–1 season. Yost had plans to stay in Palo Alto for another year, until the board at Stanford foolishly enacted a rule that barred any non-alumnus from holding a coaching position. Just think how differently the entire landscape of college football might look currently without that decision.

So, in 1901, what was Stanford's loss became Michigan's gain. It also didn't hurt that Michigan offered him a salary of $2,300, which was only $200 less than what a full professor made at the time, and he only had to be on campus for half the school year. He ended up being worth every penny and then some.

The 1901 Michigan football team would go undefeated in 11 games and outscored opposing teams by the unimaginable total of 550–0, culminating in a 49–0 drubbing of the Stanford team he had coached the year before, in the first-ever Rose Bowl (it was also the very first bowl game ever played).

Fielding H. Yost, who brought greatness to the Michigan program, poses on campus at the Waterman Gym during his first season as head coach, 1901.
*Ralph Russell Tinkham Papers*
*Courtesy of Bentley Historical Library, University of Michigan.*

Things continued like this for the next three years in Ann Arbor, seeing Yost's "Point-a-Minute" teams (as they came to be known) racking up an unthinkable 56 consecutive games without a loss, and in his first five seasons at Michigan, his teams outscored their opponents 2,821 to 42.

It was also during his early years at Michigan that Yost would basically invent the concept of recruiting for the purpose of athletics, the first example being Willie Heston, a player he met while coaching at Stanford. Heston was a star running back at San Jose State Normal School (now San Jose State), and they were playing a rematch game from a tie earlier in the season with Chico State Normal School. San Jose State decided to hire Yost as the coach for that game and the two weeks leading up to it, which apparently didn't conflict with Yost's contractual duties at Stanford. In that time he became aware of Heston's immense talent as a runner, and the two of them struck up a friendship. The next season, Yost convinced Heston to enroll in graduate school at Michigan and play football for him. Heston ended up being the cornerstone of the "Point-a-Minute" teams and is regarded as one of the first truly great players. He scored 72 career touchdowns, rushed for 170 yards in that very first Rose Bowl, and became the first Wolverine two-time All-American in 1903 and 1904.

Michigan went 43–0–1 from 1901 to 1904, winning four national championships. None of the rest of Yost's teams would quite live up to those first four teams. How could they? But there were still some monumental teams and moments in the other 21 seasons he spent at the helm in Ann Arbor. They won national championships in both 1918 and 1923, and the 1925 team featured passing standout Benny Friedman and his favorite target, the legendary Bennie Oosterbaan. Yost had not coached in 1924 when he hired assistant George Little as head coach. But when Little took the University of Wisconsin athletic directorship and football coaching position in 1925, Yost returned to coach the Wolverines. He decided to hang up his coaching spurs after the 1926 season.

In 1921, Yost assumed the role of athletic director at Michigan and revolutionized college athletics as surely as he had football. He started by convincing the Board of Regents and donors to construct intramural sports facilities for all students at the university to have access to. He'd follow those efforts with constructing a new field house for the basketball and hockey teams (completed in '23), which was, of course, named after himself, and then it was on to his crowning achievement as AD, the construction of Michigan Stadium. Completed in 1927, it was (and still is) the largest sporting venue in the Western Hemisphere. It was built with the foresight that colligate athletics shouldn't be just for students and alums, but also for the surrounding communities. And was he ever right. The money generated by the revenue from football games allowed for the creation of other sports programs within the university. In essence, he'd created the earliest example of what would now be considered a modern university athletic department. Upon his retirement in 1940, he would name his then football coach, Fritz Crisler, a man who understood Yost's vision of collegiate modernity completely, as his successor. From 1921 to 1968, under the care and guidance of those two men, the blueprints for how an athletic department is to operate were drawn.

Famed sportswriter Grantland Rice once asked both Pop Warner and Yost, "Who invented the spiral pass?" Warner replied, "Yost." He then paused, and in a tongue-in-cheek manner, added, "And he invented everything else in the game … including the football."

When  all is said and done, it's not an overstatement to say that Fielding H. Yost invented modern college football and the concept of what we think of today as the business of collegiate athletics. Whatever Michigan is today is strongly connected to the vision and endeavor of Yost. And if he were able to see it today, I'm sure he'd be pleased.

## Benny Friedman to Bennie Oosterbaan Passing Combo Revolutionizes Game

When Benny Friedman first started high school at East Technical in Cleveland, Ohio, the head football coach told a short, waifish Friedman that he'd never be big enough to play football. Most teenage boys of that stature, then and now, would take that critique, turn and walk out of that coach's office, and lay to rest their boyhood dreams of gridiron glory. Not Benny Friedman. Benny decided that he'd transfer to another East Cleveland high school, Glenville High. In his senior season of 1922, Benny led the Glenville football team to the city championship.

After arriving at the University of Michigan in the fall of 1923 and completing his year on the "all-freshman team" (as was customary in those days), Benny was poised to make his impact on the 1924 team in his sophomore season. But he was again overlooked by then head coach George Little for a starting position at Benny's best position, quarterback. After Michigan suffered one of its worst losses in program history at the hands of the "Galloping Ghost" Red Grange and the rest of the Illinois Fighting Illini, a 39–14 drubbing in which Grange scored four touchdowns in 10 minutes, Coach Little was forced to reassess some things about his approach that season, one of which was inserting Friedman at right halfback. The move paid dividends as the Wolverines went on to have a 4–1 record after adding Friedman as a starter.

At the conclusion of the 1924 season, Little departed Michigan for a job as the athletic director and head football coach at the University of Wisconsin. Wolverines athletic director Fielding H. Yost, who had established Michigan football as a powerhouse and mentored Little as his own top assistant, was left with an inadequate amount of time to find a proper replacement. Yost came out of his brief coaching retirement to assume the job at the helm of Michigan football once again.

Yost's 1925 team came in with a different look from the previous season. For starters, he'd moved Friedman from right halfback to quarterback. And in the fledgling years of the passing game in the sport, Friedman had a new target to throw to. He was a young Dutchman from Muskegon, Michigan, by the name of Bennie Oosterbaan.

The Wolverines opened the season at home against sister school, Michigan State. That game marked the first time that what would come to be known as "The Benny to Bennie Show" ever connected for a touchdown. The Wolverines would go on to win, 39–0.

The following week saw the Indiana Hoosiers come to town only to be embarrassed, 63–0. It was a game in which Friedman single-handedly accounted for 44 of the Michigan points scored. He threw five touchdown passes, ran for a 55-yard score, and converted eight point-after-touchdown kicks.

In the third week of the season, Friedman would have his chance to show his old coach, George Little, just what he had overlooked with him at quarterback when Michigan traveled to Madison to take on the Wisconsin Badgers. Friedman would leave "little" doubt (no pun intended) as to his prowess at the position as the Wolverines left Madison with a convincing 21–0 victory.

Friedman took complete control of the game on the first play from scrimmage. He faked a pass to Oosterbaan, who was sprinting downfield, and instead threw a 62-yard touchdown pass to right halfback Bruce Gregory. Friedman then did it with his legs on an 85-yard kickoff return for a touchdown and finished the scoring with a touchdown pass to Oosterbaan.

After the win in Madison, the stage was set for one the most highly-anticipated games in years, the rematch between Michigan and the Red Grange-led Fighting Illini. The Wolverines would have their revenge that day, holding Illinois scoreless and holding Grange to just 56 yards on 25 carries. The only points scored that day came on a 25-yard Friedman field goal that was set up by an Oosterbaan interception.

Two weeks later, Michigan would suffer its only loss of the season to Northwestern at Chicago's Soldier Field. The game was played in a driving rain, in temperatures that were barely above freezing—a miserable day by all accounts. It's said that some portions of the field had mud that was half a foot deep. The game ended 3–2 and ended up costing Michigan a national championship.

Friedman and Oosterbaan were both selected as All-Americans at the end of the season, and Yost would maintain until his dying day that the 1925 Michigan team was, "the greatest football team I ever coached."

(Left to Right) All-America receiver Bennie Oosterbaan, Coach Fielding H. Yost, and All-America quarterback Benny Friedman share a moment.
*Photo by Rentschler's Studio, Ann Arbor, Michigan. Courtesy of Bentley Historical Library, University of Michigan.*

The 1926 season, though not quite as impressive as the previous, still saw the Wolverines finish with just one loss, 10–0 to the eventual national champion, Navy (incidentally, a team that they'd completely dismantled in '25), in a game which saw the first touchdown scored on the Michigan defense since the 1924 season. They'd go on to grab a come-from-behind victory over Ohio State in Columbus and beat Minnesota for the second time that season (yes, you read that correctly, twice in one season).

But once again, the Wolverines fell just short of the mark, finishing No. 2 in the country for the second straight season. They did, however, win a second consecutive Big Ten championship, and Friedman was the recipient of the 1926 Big Ten Most Valuable Player Award, the *Chicago Tribune*'s Silver Football. Friedman and Oosterbann would be selected to the All-American team for a second straight year as well, but it would be the last that they'd both play together for Michigan.

Friedman would go on to revolutionize professional football in the NFL, most notably in his time with the New York Giants (1929–31), who were a four-year-old franchise struggling to put spectators in seats at the time of his arrival. Benny was noted as the "NFL's first great passer" on his Pro Football Hall of Fame induction plaque and became one of the young league's main attractions. In fact, there are some who think that if it weren't for Friedman, the New York Giants might not exist today.

After his playing days were over, Friedman began his coaching career at City College of New York until his tenure was interrupted by World War II. He volunteered for the Navy and served as a lieutenant in the Pacific arena.

Friedman returned to athletics when he was named as the first athletic director and first head football coach at Brandeis University, a post he would hold for ten years. Friedman was also a member of the very first class to be inducted into the College Football Hall of Fame in 1951.

Oosterbaan's athletic career at Michigan came to an end in 1927. When it was all said and done, he had been selected as a three-time All-American football player (the first to do so, and along with Anthony Carter, one of two in program history), a two time All-American basketball player and was also an All-Big Ten baseball selection.

Oosterbaan was inducted into the College Football Hall of Fame in 1954, but he would decline to play in both the NFL and Major League Baseball due to religious beliefs (he was a member of the Dutch Reformed Church, strict observers of the Sabbath, and are not allowed to work or play sports on Sundays). He instead went straight into coaching. He started as an assistant on the Michigan football team but would also coach basketball and baseball at Michigan. In his first year as the Wolverines' head football coach, he would win the 1948 national championship.

He remained in the Michigan athletic department in some capacity until his retirement in 1972.

He passed away in 1990 at the age of eighty-four, and legend has it that his ashes, for one reason or another, were given to the great Michigan tight end Ron Kramer, who'd played for Oosterbaan and revered him. As the story goes, Kramer proceeded to take Bennie's ashes on a tour of Oosterbaan's favorite places in Ann Arbor. He first took them to Bennie's favorite watering hole and bought a round for the two of them. From there, Kramer traveled to the University of Michigan golf course and dumped half of Bennie's ashes at his favorite hole (it's not known which hole, however) and from there went across Stadium Boulevard to Bennie's most favorite place on earth, The Big House itself, and dumped the remaining ashes in the tunnel that leads the Maize and Blue out onto the field. So it is there that he rests. He gave his life to the institution of Michigan athletics, so it's only fitting that what remained of his physical body was melded with a place that represents a near spiritual tradition practiced by millions over the decades, a tradition that was both made and preserved by pillars like Oosterbaan and Friedman.

## Michigan Stadium: The Vision and Building of the Big House

Michigan Stadium is a one-of-a-kind sports venue built in 1927 on what was once the Miller family farm in an area southwest of campus.

The stadium's history was best summed up by Wolverines radio play-by-play man Bob Ufer, who referred to it before every home game as "the hole that Yost dug, Crisler paid for, [Don] Canham carpeted, and Schembechler filled."

Every one of those men Ufer noted were both a highly-successful coach and athletic director at the University of Michigan. Each of them upgraded not only the athletic department but the stadium that came to be known as the Big House.

It all began with the "hole" dug by Fielding H. Yost, the coach of the Wolverines' "Point-a-Minute" teams that won national championships and inspired the sustained greatness. He saw the need to replace 42,000-seat Ferry Field to expand seating capacity.

There was a stadium-building boom in the 1920s when spectator sports first exploded in popularity. Just as the New York Yankees needed to house the additional fan base that turned out for Babe Ruth, Michigan needed more seats to meet the demand for the excitement created by the All-American passing combination of Benny Friedman to Bennie Oosterbaan.

Yost was both the coach and athletic director when he spearheaded the push to get his dream stadium built between 1924 and 1926. But there was opposition to the 80,000-seat structure he proposed coming from those who believed the academic mission of the school was being distorted. Robert Angell, a professor of sociology and former Wolverine tennis star, openly questioned Michigan entering the "stadium building race" that conference foes Ohio State, Minnesota, Illinois, and Northwestern were joining.

The University Senate tabled the building plan—which also included an expansion of the entire athletic campus that would impact basically every Wolverine team and recreational facilities—but Yost continued actively working on the engineering details of the stadium and promoting his vision in the media and in public forums.

A committee headed by Edmund Day, Dean of the School of Business, was formed at the request of the University Senate to study the building of a mammoth football stadium. They issued the "Day Report" in January 1926, calling for the building of a stadium "with the utmost simplicity. No attempt should be made to give it the form of a monument or memorial."

In other words, it would not resemble Memorial Stadium at the University of Illinois, built in 1923 with 200 ornate columns bearing the engraved names of Illinois men and women who gave their lives in World War I.

That "utmost simplicity" mandate likely led to the decision to dig that "hole" in the ground to build a basically underground stadium, a concept not unlike installing an in-ground swimming pool. That construction approach also played into fitting the selected terrain located in a valley.

A story on the building of Michigan Stadium written for the University of Michigan's Bentley Historical Library said the Day Report was "probably the most significant single document in the development of Michigan's modern athletic program," and included the University Golf Course and Yost Field House, a multipurpose facility Yost invented that was replicated across the country and eventually transformed into Yost Ice Arena.

Yost wanted the greatest capacity manageable for the stadium, and that caused a debate. He foresaw a day when 125,000 and even 150,000 seats would be needed to meet ticket demands. That was then perceived as unrealistic but has been approached. A record for pro or college football attendance was set when 115,109 filled Michigan Stadium on September 7, 2013, for Michigan's thrilling, 41–30, night game victory over Notre Dame. That record stood for three years before over 150,000 fans watched Tennessee and Virginia Tech play at Bristol Motor Speedway.

However, that attendance total against the Fighting Irish in 2013 remains a record for a game played at an on-campus or regularly-scheduled home stadium.

As a concession to Yost in the plans approved for a 72,000-seat stadium, the footings were constructed to permit a 100,000-seat stadium expansion in the future. That move was crucial to the stadium being able to someday reach and exceed that figure.

The stadium was originally planned to be built where the University of Michigan Golf Course is located, but instead, a 16-acre tract of land was purchased for $239,000 across from there on what is now called Stadium Boulevard. It was located across the railroad tracks, which still exist there, from Ferry Field.

Yost hired Osborn Engineering of Cleveland, which also designed Yankee Stadium, Fenway Park, Navin Field in Detroit that became Tiger Stadium, Chicago's Comiskey Park, and others. Bernard Green, the chief architect for Michigan Stadium, graduated from Michigan's College of Engineering in 1891.

The new stadium's location was to be in a valley where Allen's Creek, since diverted underground, once flowed. Excavation of the land began in August 1926, and lights were installed to allow around-the-clock work. Steam shovels, trucks, and horse-and-wagon haulers were used.

The discovery of natural springs caused a challenge, though. Construction was nearly halted, but a Detroit Fire Department pump was used to help remove the water in what already was a naturally swampy area. Extensive drainage was required.

Concrete pouring began May 9, 1927. Some 11,000 yards of concrete, 440 tons of reinforcing steel, and 31,000 square feet of wire mesh went into the construction of the stadium, modeled in part after the Yale Bowl but more oblong than round in its design.

That June, more than 22 miles of redwood plank seats were installed. A four-leaf clover was planted in the field sod, and the press box and locker rooms were constructed.

The project came in on time and on budget, costing $1,131,733.36—one-third less than the $1.7 million required for Illinois's Memorial Stadium.

The first game—a 33–0 win over Ohio Wesleyan on October 1, 1927—was played in a heavy rainstorm, and the official attendance was 17,483.

Three weeks later, 84,401 packed the stadium for the 21–0 dedication game victory over Ohio State. Yost's request for an additional 10,000 bleacher seats being constructed was approved to increase capacity in what was the first of many expansion efforts.

Aerial photo of Michigan Stadium during the opening game in what became known as "The Big House" against Ohio Wesleyan in 1927.
*A.B.C. Airline Corp. photo. Courtesy of Bentley Historical Library, University of Michigan.*

Capacity reached 85,753 in 1928, and rows of stands were added above-ground over the years. It rose to 97,239 in 1949, when former football coach and then athletic director Fritz Crisler went about paying off the stadium, as per Ufer's stadium history line.

Michigan Stadium went over the mark Yost—then dead for exactly ten years—had envisioned by reaching 101,101 as capacity in 1956. As an aside, influential Detroit alumni pushed to have it renamed Yost Stadium in 1945 but gave up their petition when Yost himself said he did not want that.

Don Canham, who replaced Crisler, "carpeted" the place in 1969, adding the artificial Tartan Turf that had become popular in NFL stadiums. But his greatest legacy—exceeding even his business acumen—was the January 1969 hiring of Schembechler, who "filled" a stadium that had averaged just 67,991 in 1968.

Schembechler's teams won and captured the imagination of Michigan fans. The Wolverines have attracted at least 100,000 every game since November 8, 1975.

Bo Schembechler (left) and All-America offensive tackle Dan Dierdorf examine a new turf shoe designed for the artificial surface installed at Michigan Stadium.
*Courtesy of Bentley Historical Library, University of Michigan.*

Canham, who died in 2005, said hiring Schembechler was the "turning point" of his career, but his marketing genius also contributed to huge crowds.

He promoted tailgating as a way to attract families to games and drew ire for unabashed promotion. Canham had a plane fly over Tiger Stadium during the 1968 World Series to sell tickets and brought in the San Diego Chicken and the Clydesdales. He sent slick brochures to homes via mail, hawking tickets and Wolverine merchandise from coffee cups and bumper stickers to T-shirts and everything in between.

The former Michigan track high-jumper coached 11 Big Ten championship track and field teams, built his own million-dollar athletic gear company from the ground up, and was a born promoter.

Canham expanded and licensed the Michigan brand and put millions of dollars in the athletic department coffers for years to come when, in 1982, he got the Board of Regents to register the Block M trademark and create a nation-wide licensing trend in college athletics that became a billion-dollar industry.

He was arguably the most significant college athletic director in history.

Michigan Stadium capacity rose to 101,701 in 1973, 102,501 in 1992, and 107,501 in 1998, and the building of eighty-three luxury suites and other expansion in a $226 million renovation boosted it to 109,901 in 2010.

Construction adjustments needed to improve accessibility under the Americans with Disabilities Act caused for the elimination of seats to widen aisles and install hand railings, reducing capacity to 107,601 in 2015.

The one constant in capacity totals since 1956 is the "1" at the end as requested by Crisler and continued in honor of the man who won national championships as a coach before serving as athletic director from 1941 to 1968.

Michigan Stadium has had the highest average attendance figure in college football in every season since 1974 with the exceptions of 1997 and 2014.

The Big House that Yost, Crisler, Canham, and Schembechler—who also happened to maintain amazing athletic department continuity in ninety years with just four directors—combined to envision, build, renovate, and fill to capacity what became a legendary, must-see venue.

When the place opened in 1927, John Miller was an attendant at Gate No. 6. He remained there for home games over the next fifty years, nearly a decade after Canham and Schembechler took the stadium built where his father once erected a farmhouse to unprecedented heights.

(Left to Right) Coaches Harry Kipke, Fritz Crisler, Bennie Oosterbaan, Bump Elliott, and Bo Schembechler pose in Michigan Stadium in 1969. *Courtesy of Bentley Historical Library, University of Michigan.*

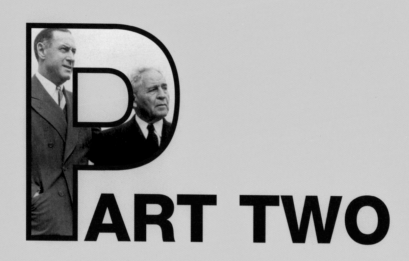

# PART TWO

# CRISLER AND THE MODERN ERA

# Tom Harmon, 1940 Heisman Trophy Winner

In 1937, then Michigan athletic director and former coaching legend Fielding H. Yost described a brawny high school senior from Gary, Indiana, named Tom Harmon as "the greatest high school athlete of the year." At that point, the Michigan football program was going through some lean years and wasn't quite the prime destination for top football talent that it had been in the previous decade. As providence would have it, it just so happened that Harmon's football coach at Horace Mann High School was a former Wolverine football player named Douglas Kerr. Harmon would enroll at the University of Michigan in the fall of '37 and play his first season on the freshman team. The Wolverine varsity team would go 4–4 in what would end up being coach Harry Kipke's last year at the helm of the struggling program. The tides of fortune were about to change, however.

The 1938 season saw the arrival in Ann Arbor of Fritz Crisler, an already established coach who played for and coached alongside the great Amos Alonzo Stagg at the University of Chicago. Crisler's last coaching stop had been at Princeton, where he'd led the Tigers to two perfect seasons in '33 and '35. The first of many innovations that Crisler would make at Michigan would be the introduction of the now famous winged helmet; an idea that would seem to have a Samson-like effect on Tom Harmon, who was now in his first year on the varsity squad as a sophomore. The Wolverines would lose only one game in the first year of the new era of Crisler and his scintillating sophomore, going 6–1–1 and closing out the season with an 18–0 victory in Columbus. Harmon would score a touchdown in the first quarter of that game that became the first points scored by Michigan against Ohio State since 1933, and the powerful, fleet-footed halfback would go on to receive All-Conference honors in his very first varsity season.

The Wolverines would have a slightly above average season the following year, going 6–2. They lost games to Illinois and Minnesota, but the season was certainly not without highlights. In the second game of the year, they beat Iowa, 27–7, with Harmon scoring every point for the Michigan offense that day. Their 85–0 dismantling of the University of Chicago basically led to the dissolution of the once dominant football program at the end of the '39 season. And in the final game, the Wolverines came from behind to beat the sixth-ranked Buckeyes, 21–14, after Ohio State had led early, 14–0. It was Harmon who spearheaded the comeback and played a direct role in all 21 points scored. At season's end, Harmon was

Part Two

selected to the All-American team, posting some very impressive numbers. He finished the season with 868 yards on 129 carries, for an average of 6.7 yards per carry. His 108 yards per game were the best in the country, along with his 102 points on 14 touchdowns, 15 extra points, and one field goal. He would finish as runner-up to Nile Kinnick of Iowa in the Heisman voting that year, which, if you ask me, was a total snub. Harmon's numbers are far more impressive than Kinnick's, and then you factor in that Michigan and Harmon completely eviscerated Iowa and Kinnick when the two faced off head-to-head that season. But in those days it was customary to give the award to the best senior in the country, which Kinnick may have very well been that year. However, had that not been the practice, Michigan would, and should, have had the first two-time Heisman Trophy winner.

The 1940 season picked up right where it had left off for Harmon, and then some. In the opening game at Cal, he ran for four touchdowns, kicked four extra points, and threw for another touchdown. His performance that day was electric. No one on the field seemed capable of tackling him, including a Cal fan that leapt onto the field and attempted to tackle Harmon in the end zone after a touchdown run. Sadly, the attempted tackle by the more than likely inebriated fan is what most people recall about the game, but it was truly one of the greatest single-game performances in the history of college football.

The following week, Harmon would score all three touchdowns and kick all three extra points in a 21–14 defeat of Michigan State, and after only two games, he had already racked up a total of 49 points by himself. I think most coaches (especially back in those days) would be happy if their entire offense scored 49 points in two games against respectable competition. After Week 4 of that season, the Harmon point tally was up to 80, and he was well on his way to claiming the Heisman Trophy.

Michigan suffered its only loss of 1940 at the hands of Minnesota, the eventual national champions. It was a game played in mucky, early November Minnesota conditions that saw Harmon give what was probably the worst performance of his career. The Wolverines twice had the ball inside the Golden Gophers' 5 yard line, only to come away empty-handed. The first was a 4th-and-1 at the goal line that Harmon lost his footing on, coming up just short. The second was an errant Harmon pass that was picked off in the end zone. And to make the loss extra excruciating, one that I'm sure Harmon lost plenty of sleep over, he threw the game's only touchdown pass but then missed the ensuing extra point. Minnesota would answer with seven points before the half, but neither team could manage to score a single point in the second half on what had to become one sorry excuse for a football field. Michigan's greatest weapon had been neutralized by Mother Nature, and the Gophers eked out a 7–6 win.

In what would be the final game of the season and the final game of Tom Harmon's illustrious college football career, the Wolverines traveled down to Columbus and completely owned the Buckeyes in a 40–0 thrashing that led to the forced resignation of Ohio State head coach Francis Schmidt. Harmon put up video game numbers that day, running for three touchdowns, passing for two touchdowns, and kicking four extra points … and just for good measure, he punted three times for a 50-yard average and picked off three passes on defense. If there was any doubt as to who the Heisman Trophy winner should be going into that game, it was crystal clear afterward. Even Buckeyes fans knew who the best player in the land was that year and showed their appreciation at the end of the game, giving Harmon a

Tom Harmon leaves the field with Wolverines assistant coach Earl Martineau after a command performance at Ohio Stadium, where he received a standing ovation from Buckeyes fans in his final game for Michigan in 1940. *Courtesy of Bentley Historical Library, University of Michigan.*

standing ovation, the only Michigan player to ever receive that honor in Ohio Stadium. It was a rare showing of class and sportsmanship for that bunch … in any generation.

Harmon, known as "Old 98" for his iconic uniform number, would go on to win the Heisman by a landslide, becoming Michigan's very first recipient. He was also given the Maxwell Award and voted the Athlete of the Year by the Associated Press, beating out Detroit Tigers slugging great Hank Greenberg. He bested Red Grange's single-season touchdown record for the Big Ten by two with 33 and led the nation in scoring for the second consecutive season.

Harmon was taken first overall by the Chicago Bears in the 1941 NFL Draft, but in the fledgling years of the league, the prospect of playing professionally wasn't nearly as appealing. The money was small change compared to what players make today, and franchises were closing up shop almost as quickly as you could say, "Want to come to Hollywood and make a movie about your life?" which is just what Harmon decided to do, in lieu of playing professional football. The movie was titled *Harmon of Michigan*, and there's a reason why the vast majority of even the most diehard of Michigan fans haven't seen it. It's regarded as one of the worst sports movies ever made. In his defense, he did have some training as a performer (mostly in radio), but it was a half-baked attempt by Columbia Pictures to cash in on the widespread fame that Harmon was enjoying. You can't knock a kid for chasing his dreams. Shortly after the film's release, the Japanese bombed Pearl Harbor, and all of Harmon's plans and dreams were put on hold. He enlisted in the United States Army Air Corps, and less than a year later, he was commissioned as a second lieutenant, Army bomber pilot. In April of 1943, a bomber piloted by Harmon crashed in a South American jungle while en route from Arizona to North Africa. Heavy rain and turbulence caused the crash that day, of which Harmon was the lone survivor. He wandered for four days through the jungles of what is now Suriname and was eventually rescued by natives who days later brought him to a base of the Antilles Air Command in an outrigger canoe. As traumatic as that experience may have been, there was no time to rest. The future of the free world hung in the balance, and every able-bodied man was needed to fight the Axis. He was shipped to North Africa, where he had a brief assignment, this time as a P-38 fighter pilot, before being sent off to fight with the 449th Fighter Squadron in the Pacific arena. In the summer of '43, Harmon's P-38 fighter was shot down by a Japanese Zero in a dogfight over the Yangtze River in China. He survived the crash and was fortunate enough to be found by Chinese guerrillas who were fighting off occupying Japanese forces. They escorted him out of enemy territory and back to safety. Harmon was awarded the Purple Heart and the Silver Star, and in April of 1945, he was promoted to the rank of captain. He was discharged from the Army at the end of the war later that year. To say that Harmon was lucky to survive the war would be quite an understatement.

Shortly after returning stateside from the war, Harmon married movie actress Elyse Knox in a ceremony that took place at St. Mary's Student Parish in Ann Arbor. After the war's end, Tom would go to work for WJR radio in Detroit, covering Michigan football games, before being bitten by the football bug again and signing a two-year deal with the Los Angeles Rams. It's speculated that Harmon only signed the contract to pay off a debt from a previous professional football contract that he'd never made good on, but I think it probably had more to do with being married to a movie actress who wanted to be where movies are made, and Harmon himself wanting to see how much he had left in the football tank. Which in the case of the latter, it was determined pretty quickly that there wasn't as much left as he may have thought. War and being away from the game for so long had taken a toll on his body, and after the two years of very minimal contribution to the Rams, his playing days were over in 1947.

After football, Harmon went on to enjoy huge success as a radio and television announcer. He worked at different points in his career for CBS, ABC Radio, and NBC. While at NBC, he worked in the booth on some of the earliest televised broadcasts of the Rose Bowl.

Tom and Elyse had three children, all of whom would go on to be people of note in and around Hollywood. His son, Mark, was the most visible, playing football at UCLA and later having a successful career as a television actor.

Tom Harmon's legacy in the world of college football is so vast that only a select few players can even be mentioned in the same sentence. The athleticism, power, and grace with which he carried the football were so aesthetically pleasing to watch that you'd believe someone had choreographed it.

Harmon passed away in March of 1990, a little more than a year before Michigan had its second Heisman Trophy winner, Desmond Howard.

# Coach Fritz Crisler

In the young life of every protégé, there must be an encounter with a master if their potential is to be realized—a virtuoso who guides their talents until the hand of the protégé is so certain of itself, it only knows its own inner direction.

Herbert Orin Crisler was born in 1899 on a small farm in Earlville, Illinois, a tiny village about 70 miles west of Chicago. By his own accounts, he was a waifish, bookish kid who concentrated intently on his studies. After graduating with exceptional marks from Mendota High School in 1918, he was awarded an academic scholarship to the University of Chicago. In the fall of '18, as a freshman pre-med student, he went out exploring the campus and happened upon the varsity football practice. As he stood on the sideline, taking it all in, he failed to notice a sweep play heading right in his direction. A backpedaling coach unwittingly plowed into the young Crisler, knocking them both over, and when he had collected himself, Crisler arose to see that it was none other than legendary head coach Amos Alonzo Stagg.

In a 1964 interview with *Sports Illustrated*, Crisler recalled the meeting as follows: "As we picked ourselves up, he saw by my cap, that I was a freshman so he said, 'Why aren't you out for freshman football?' I had gained some weight by that time, but I told Mr. Stagg that I had never played football. He said, 'You ought to be out anyway with the rest of your classmates.' So I reported the next afternoon, got a uniform, and Pat Page, the freshman coach, put me in a scrimmage. I took a terrible pounding. That evening I turned in my uniform. About 10 days later I was crossing the quadrangle and I saw Mr. Stagg coming along on his bicycle. I ducked my head, but he spotted me and stopped. He said, 'Weren't you out for football?' I said I had been, but I had quit because I didn't know anything about the game. I'll never forget the look of scorn Mr. Stagg gave me. 'Well,' he said, 'I never thought you'd be a quitter!'"

But Crisler didn't realize until right that moment that he was far from done. He went back to practice that next day, and the course his life would take was set. He would go on to earn nine varsity letters in three sports—three in baseball, three in basketball, and three on Coach Stagg's football team, where he even received All-American honors.

At some point in Crisler's sophomore year, Stagg began referring to Crisler as Fritz. There was a famous Austrian violinist of the time named, Fritz Kreisler, and Crisler himself always stated it was to mock him for fumbling the ball three times in a row one practice. But my read, and I'm sure Crisler knew the same deep down, was that it was a term of endearment. The master had found his protégé, and the protégé, his master.

Upon completing undergraduate studies, Crisler enrolled in the medical school at the University of Chicago, but would soon be forced to drop out due to a lack of personal funds. He was offered a position as an assistant coach on the football team by Stagg himself, and within a few short years under Stagg's tutelage, he was offered a position as the head football coach at the University of Minnesota at the ripe young age of twenty-five. He asked his mentor for counsel, and Stagg said, "Fritz, you're not ready to fly." But when Minnesota came calling again six years later, and this time offered him not only the head coaching job but the athletic director's position as well, Stagg's advice was, "Now you're ready to fly, Fritz. Go to it."

In his two years as head coach at Minnesota (1930–31), Crisler would post a 10–7–1 record and become a mentor himself to a young man who played the guard position by the name of Biggie Munn. Munn would go on to coach on Crisler's staff at Michigan and eventually take what he'd learned from Crisler and use it as the building blocks for the first formidable football teams that Michigan State had ever fielded. The Spartans would enjoy the greatest era of football in their history under Munn in the 1950s.

By 1932, Crisler had moved on to Princeton, where he compiled a record of 35–9–5 in his six seasons as head coach with his '33 and '35 teams each going a perfect 9–0 and claiming a share of national titles those years.

It was during his time at Princeton that Crisler first came up with the idea of a painted, winged helmet, but it wasn't until he brought the idea with him to Ann Arbor in 1938 that the winged helmet became the indelible, maize and blue image that has become synonymous with Michigan football.

The Wolverine football program improved quickly under Crisler and by 1940 had produced the program's first Heisman Trophy winner in halfback Tom Harmon. The following year saw the famed architect of Michigan athletics, Fielding H. Yost, retire as athletic director, and Crisler became his handpicked successor. With all his responsibilities both on and off the football field, it's quite remarkable that Crisler remained on the tactical forefront of the game. At the outbreak of war in 1941, college football saw many of its players go overseas to serve their country. As a result, teams were greatly diminished in their number of players and a change to the substitution rule was enacted. The reason that eleven men played most of the game back then was because coming out of a game meant that you had to sit out until the start of the next quarter. But when the rule changed to unlimited substitutions because of a lack of players, Crisler saw an opportunity. It took him a few years to work out the kinks, but in a game against Army in 1945, Crisler unveiled his famed "Split Squad" of eleven men playing mostly on defense and eleven mostly on offense. It took him a couple more seasons to perfect it, but by 1947, the Wolverines were firing on all cylinders. No one had ever seen anything like it, and football reporters around the country dubbed them "The Mad Magicians."

The speed and sleight-of-hand tactics that they employed on offense left defenses dumbfounded, and they finished the season undefeated (10–0), including a 49–0 trouncing of USC in the Rose Bowl. Crisler would retire from coaching after the '47 season and finish with a 71–16–3 record (.805) at Michigan, second only to Yost (.833) in winning percentage among those who coached more than three seasons.

Wolverines coach Fritz Crisler at practice.
*Courtesy of Bentley Historical Library, University of Michigan.*

Part Two

Crisler would go down in history as one of the most visionary and accomplished coaches of his era, or any other for that matter. Though, it was his tenure as a full-time athletic director that would prove to be his most trailblazing work.

He would take the already gargantuan Michigan Stadium, with its capacity of 85,752, and expand it to 97,239 in 1949. Seven years later, in 1956, he'd again expand the capacity to an almost unimaginable number of 101,001. He was asked many times who the extra seat was for, but it would always remain a secretive gesture towards a figure that outsiders could only guess at.

In his time at the helm of the Michigan athletic department, his attention to sports other than football, baseball, and basketball were also revolutionary for the time. In Crisler's twenty-seven years as athletic director, his sports programs achieved an unprecedented level of success. The hockey team won seven national championships, the men's swimming team won six national championships, the football team won a national championship, six Big Ten titles, and three Rose Bowls, the baseball team won two national championships and ten Big Ten titles, the basketball team twice appeared in the Final Four and won four Big Ten titles, the men's gymnastics team won a national championship and seven Big Ten titles, the men's tennis team won a national championship and twelve Big Ten titles, the wrestling team won seventeen Big Ten titles, and the track and field team won eighteen Big Ten titles.

His last great achievement as athletic director before retiring in 1968 was the construction of a new basketball arena. The University Events Building, as it was first known, opened in 1967 after the success of the basketball team (featuring the great Cazzie Russell) created a higher demand for tickets than Yost Field House (now Yost Ice Arena) could accommodate. The 13,684 seat arena (now 12,707) was designed by one of Crisler's former players, Dan Dworsky, and was renamed Crisler Arena in 1970 to honor the man who'd done so much to make Michigan athletics what they are today.

The breadth of Crisler's legacy is in some ways immeasurable. His impact on the way the sport of football is played and on modern collegiate athletics is perhaps larger than any other figure of his era. We're talking about a man who proposed the two-point conversion and suggested widening goal posts to increase the number of field goals attempted. He served on the college football rules committee for several decades and basically was the first AD to fully understand the financial potential of college sports at that point in time. The successor he chose, Don Canham, was a man who understood Crisler's vision 100 percent and would go on to hire Bo Schembechler in his first year on the job. Years later, Bo often spoke of the personal influence that Crisler had on him. He regularly visited Crisler at his home, and the two became close friends. The master had found yet another protégé, creating a program that has a direct lineage, a certain specific way of doing things. It's the essence of what being a "Michigan Man" is all about. It's a time-tested, time-honored way of doing things. It's a way that you carry yourself through life. And much of that comes from Crisler.

Fritz Crisler is certainly one of four on the Mount Rushmore of Michigan football and is definitely among the most influential figures in the history of the sport.

Michigan coach Fritz Crisler poses in 1947 with his mentor, Amos Alonzo Stagg, who signed the photo: "Affectionate regards from your old coach and friend, Amos Alonzo Stagg."
*From H.O. Crisler Papers Courtesy of Bentley Historical Library, University of Michigan.*

# The "Mad Magicians"

In 1947 there were thousands and thousands of young men who had recently returned home from Europe and Asia. They were coming home no doubt forever changed by their experiences in war. In many cases, their lives and plans had been put on hold so that they could fulfill their duty to defend the country, and the young men of the Michigan football program were no exception. There were several players who served bravely and returned to their beloved state and their beloved school to resume their goals that had been set out years prior. In the grand scheme of things, I doubt that football held the place of importance it did in their youth before their eyes were made to see so much. But I doubt that it had ever been as much fun, either. The young men of the Michigan football program returned home to Ann Arbor focused and driven and produced an on-field product that was rare before that season and even rarer since.

Bob Chappuis had played at Michigan in 1942 and was one of those Wolverines returning from World War II. He was an aerial gunner and radio operator on an Army Air Forces B-52 bomber shot down over German-occupied Italy in February 1945. He parachuted to safety and was hidden from the Nazis in a barn in the countryside by Italian resistance for three months before the war ended in Europe.

When returning to Michigan, he initially wondered about how much he wanted to play football again.

"I didn't think I wanted to get myself all excited and lose sleep the night before a game," Chappuis (CHAPP-ee-us) told Rob Newell in *From Playing Field to Battlefield*, published in 2006.

Though he played well at halfback in 1946, Chappuis really hit stride the next year as an integral part of Coach Fritz Crisler's "Mad Magicians," who turned ball-handling into an art.

Crisler also adopted a system in 1947 that would revolutionize the sport and would eventually become the norm for most levels of football. He decided to split his team into offensive and defensive squads. And with the exception of two players who played on both sides of the ball, the Wolverines were the first football team to fully embrace the split-squad or two-platoon concept. Crisler would also have the talent and the time with the offense that season to implement a more daring, breakneck style of play. Their single-wing formation was filled with sets and plays meant to keep a defense bewildered as to which Wolverine player even had the ball. There really isn't a modern offense that compares as far as deception goes. They would line up with four men in the backfield and shift those players in one fashion or another on almost every play. Direct snaps could go to any of the four depending on the formation. The plays were filled with misdirection, play fakes, and just flat out hiding who had the football. This brand of offense would earn the team that moniker of "The Mad Magicians," and only two games of their undefeated season would be decided by less than 21 points.

It became clear fairly early in the 1947 season that it was a two horse race for the national championship between the Wolverines and the Fighting Irish of Notre Dame. With both teams steamrolling the vast majority of their respective opponents, the two teams leapfrogged one another for the number one spot in the rankings seemingly every week. And even though Michigan would close out its undefeated regular season by shutting out Ohio State, 21–0, on November 22, it would be jumped by Notre Dame, which closed out its regular season December 6 by beating the No. 3 Southern Cal Trojans, 38–7.

Now, in today's game, the stage would just be getting set for some classic play-off matchups. But in those days the national champion was crowned the week after every regular season game had been played, and bowl games were just a nice vacation that you went on as a reward for a well-played season and a chance to claim some bragging rights for your program and conference. The first-place votes at the end of the regular season gave Notre Dame the slightest of edges, but to further complicate the argument as to who was more deserving of the crown, Michigan would travel to Pasadena for the first time since 1902 to play the same Trojans team that the Fighting Irish had just annihilated.

The 1948 Rose Bowl turned out to be a clinic on the game of football that the Wolverines would put on for USC, beating them 49–0.

Chappuis was a star in that win over the Trojans, passing for 188 yards and two touchdowns and rushing for 91 yards. It was the capper to a special season, during which he ran and passed for a combined 1,395 yards and 18 touchdowns. He also appeared on the cover of *TIME* magazine on November 3, 1947.

When Chappuis died in 2012, backfield mate Bump Elliott told the *New York Times*, "For a single-wing offense, we threw the ball an awful lot. It was more passing and deception than power. The key was Bob's ability to pass so well."

Southern Cal was no match for Michigan's offense or defense. The Wolverines had a winning margin that was 18 points greater than the Fighting Irish managed against the same team just weeks earlier. And if you add in the fact that against common opponents—Pittsburgh, Northwestern and USC—Michigan beat all three by more points than Notre Dame, a pretty convincing argument could be made that the Associated Press chose the wrong team for the title that year. An unofficial revote was conducted by a portion of the AP voters after the Rose Bowl that had Michigan coming out on top as national champion, but it was too late. The official vote had already been cast, and Michigan would have to play second fiddle … at least for that season.

There were, however, plenty of individual accolades to go around for the Wolverines of 1947. Chappuis was selected as first team All-American and finished second in the Heisman Trophy voting to Note Dame quarterback Johnny Lujack. Bump Elliott was also selected as a first team All-American as well as being named MVP of the Big Nine Conference (as it was known then before Michigan State had joined). Len Ford, Bob Mann, and J. T. White were all named to the second team All-America list.

Chappuis, Ford, Alvin Wistert, Pete Elliott, and Bump Elliott would all go on to be inducted into either the college or pro football hall of fame. The maize and blue No. 11 worn by Wistert and before him his brothers, Albert and Francis, who also were All-American tackles bound for the College Football Hall of Fame, has been retired at Michigan.

The "Mad Magicians" Michigan backfield of (left to right) Bump Elliott, Howard Yerges, Jack Weisenburger, and Bob Chappuis sprint on the grass field at Fisher Stadium. They were known for their deceptive ball-handling, speed, and quickness.
*Courtesy of Bentley Historical Library, University of Michigan.*

The Michigan football program underwent major changes between the 1947 and 1948 seasons. For one, their esteemed head coach stepped down. Crisler also was the athletic director and would hand the reins of his football team over to long-time assistant and legendary Wolverines receiver Bennie Oosterbaan.

Oosterbaan was well-known in coaching circles of the time as an offensive mastermind. But it was his defense that would receive much of the accolades in his first season at the helm. After losing all four starters from his offensive backfield of the previous year, he would have to sharpen his approach. Following a narrow 13–7 victory over Michigan State to open the season, it was clear that the '48 team did not have the offensive prowess of the '47 squad. But in the following three games, the Wolverines would emerge as a defense to be reckoned with. Led by defensive tackles Alvin Wistert and Al Wahl, they would go on to shut out ranked opponents Oregon (which had future college and pro Hall of Fame quarterback Norm Van Brocklin), Purdue, and Northwestern. The offense would find its stride in the passing game, most notably through the combination of Chuck Ortmann to Dick Rifenburg. And once they had everything clicking on both sides of the ball, there was little that opposing teams could do to stop the Wolverines from taking over games.

They would travel down to Columbus, Ohio, for the final game of the '48 season with everything on the line. They beat the Buckeyes, 13–3, that day and laid claim to both the Big Nine title and the national championship, this time garnering nearly double the number of votes that second place Notre Dame would receive.

In the end, as the adage goes, it was the defense that won championships. The Wolverines held opponents to a combined total of 44 points for the entire season. That's a whopping 4.9 points per game on average. They also forced 32 turnovers (21 of them were interceptions), averaging out to 3.6 per game.

Maybe the most impressive feat from these teams is that from the last four games of the 1946 season to the end of the 1948 season, they would win a staggering 23 straight games. Rifenburg, Alvin Wistert, and Pete Elliott would all receive first team All-American honors in '48, and captain and left guard Dominic Tomasi was named the team's Most Valuable Player.

When the last page had been turned on this chapter of Michigan football, a very strong argument could be formed that these were some of the very best college teams to ever play the sport.

# Roses Bloom in the Snow Bowl

There are college football games every season which are played in less than ideal conditions.

Sometimes games have to be postponed or moved to a different locale because of weather. But of all the games that have actually been played on severely inclement days, perhaps none was more harrowing or more famous than the game played between Michigan and Ohio State on November 25, 1950, in Columbus at Ohio Stadium.

Thanksgiving Day, two days prior to "The Game" that year, was what you'd generally expect weather-wise for the Midwest that time of year—38 degrees and raining. But in the 36 hours that followed, the Midwest experienced a 30-degree drop in temperature, and to make matters worse, there was a powerful rainstorm moving north up the Atlantic coast. The extreme moisture from that storm front would meet the blistering cold air moving south from Canada and create conditions that were almost unheard of for November in central Ohio.

The conditions were so unthinkably terrible that a meeting between Michigan's head coach and athletic director (Bennie Oosterbaan and Fritz Crisler, respectively) and their Ohio State counterparts (Wes Fesler and Dick Larkins) was necessary to determine whether the game could even be played. No one knows for sure what was exchanged during this meeting, but in the end, the two teams agreed that with a conference championship on the line, the game must be played.

From the very start of the game, it was a complete punt-fest. Both teams were regularly punting on second down and even sometimes first down, depending on field position. Both teams were thinking that their best chance to get points that day would be a turnover deep in the opposition's territory. There were 45 punts in all that day, 24 by Michigan's Chuck Ortmann and 21 by OSU's Vic Janowicz, totaling 1,408 yards. It was Ohio State that got on the scoreboard first with a 38-yard field goal in the first quarter by Janowicz, who won the Heisman Trophy that year. It was a pretty astonishing kick considering that there was a foot of snow on the field and 28 mile-per-hour winds swirling around The Horseshoe. Michigan would get the game's next points after Al Wahl blocked a Janowicz punt that rolled through the back of OSU's end zone for a safety.

With 20 seconds left on the clock in the second quarter, Buckeyes coach Fesler would make a questionable decision to punt the ball on third down, deep in their own territory. Michigan's Tony Momsen blocked the punt and fell on it in the end zone for the game's only touchdown. After Harry Allis converted the point-after attempt, the Wolverines would take a 9–3 lead, and with neither team able to produce much of anything in the second half, that's the way it would end, without even a single first down from the Michigan offense.

Michigan punter Chuck Ortmann runs around the Buckeyes in the 1950 Snow Bowl game in Columbus, Ohio. *Michiganensian photo. Courtesy of Bentley Historical Library, University of Michigan.*

Michigan still needed some help that day from Northwestern if they were to win the conference title. The Wildcats faced off that same day (in much better conditions) against an Illinois team that had beaten the Wolverines earlier in the season. Michigan would get the help they needed with a 14–7 Wildcats victory, and that meant that they had won the conference outright and were heading to Pasadena.

The *Detroit Free Press* headline the next day was a classic: "The Roses that Bloom in the Snow."

The Wolverines would beat the Cal Golden Bears by a score of 14–6 in the 37th Rose Bowl game.

The 1950 Michigan-Ohio State game was the fourth in a row that Fesler and his Buckeyes had lost to the Wolverines, which spelled the end of the road for Fesler. He would be replaced the following season with a coach by the name of Wayne Woodrow Hayes.

## Ron Kramer, Tight End Prototype

Every kid who grows up playing sports grows up with a kid who seems to have been manufactured in some top-secret sports laboratory somewhere. That kid who's bigger than everyone else, stronger than everyone else, and to boot, can run faster and jump higher than everyone else, too.

Well, on the east side of Detroit in the early 1950s, that kid was Ron Kramer. Except that his athletic gifts weren't just superior, they were legendary. Kramer was a once-in-a-generation athlete in the entire state of Michigan. If he were coming out of high school today, he'd be at least a No. 3 overall recruit in the country and no doubt a five-star on every recruiting site in the universe. And if his prowess on the gridiron weren't enough, the 6-foot-3, 230-pounder was also All-State in both basketball and track and field. So when Kramer decided to make the short move from Detroit to Ann Arbor in 1953, he was able to help revive the Wolverines.

Head football coach Bennie Oosterbaan had won a national championship in his very first season in 1948, but the team had since slipped into mediocrity. Kramer would be the spark he needed to ignite the program once again. Kramer would start at end on both offense and defense in his first varsity season as a sophomore in 1954, playing in all nine games. It was apparent early on that Ron wasn't just a large kid with tons of athleticism, but also one who played with a mean streak. He quickly became known as much for his blocking and tackling as he was for his gracefulness with the ball, and he was named first team All-Big Ten at the end of his sophomore year.

Kramer would lead Michigan to its best records of the decade (7–2) and be named a first team All-American in both 1955 and 1956, his junior and senior seasons. He also was a placekicker and led the team in scoring both of those seasons and, believe it or not, did the same for the Wolverines basketball team as a junior. On the court he would rack up a total of 1,119 points in his career for a record that would stand until 1961. He also managed to find time to compete in the high jump on the track team, which at his size is pretty much unheard of, even back then. In all, he would receive nine varsity letters.

In 1957, Kramer was a fifth-round pick in the NBA Draft by the Fort Wayne Pistons, who became the Detroit Pistons later that year. But seeing as he was the fourth pick overall in the 1957 NFL Draft, he wisely decided to go that route. He had been taken by the Green Bay Packers, along with their No. 1 overall pick of Notre Dame halfback Paul Hornung, the Heisman Trophy winner. The two would go on to serve as the offensive cornerstones of Vince Lombardi's back-to-back NFL championship teams in 1961 and 1962. The offense was built around a single play, the famous "Packer Sweep" in which Kramer's blocking played a huge part in the success. Kramer would be selected as a first team All-Pro in 1962 and a second team All-Pro in 1963. He became the prototype of the modern tight end, who not only blocked but was a weapon in the passing game.

In 1965, Kramer was traded to his hometown Detroit Lions but was never really able to recapture the magic of those early years with the Packers, and in 1968 he decided that his playing days were over.

Kramer would go on to have success as a local businessman in southeastern Michigan in both the steel and advertising industries and enjoyed a number of honors bestowed upon him for his athletic achievements as a young man. He was inducted into the Michigan Sports Hall of Fame in 1971, the College Football Hall of Fame in 1978, and his No. 87 football jersey is one of six jerseys to ever be retired at Michigan.

Kramer would remain a very visible figure around the Michigan football program

Ron Kramer, an All-American tight end in 1955 and 1956, who also played defensive end, in front of Yost Field House. *Courtesy of the University of Michigan.*

for the rest of his life, and he acted as somewhat of an advisor to Coach Lloyd Carr. Carr stated that Kramer would call him every time that Michigan lost a game to offer his support. He also remained close friends with his coach and mentor, Oosterbaan, right up until Bennie's death in 1990. Kramer passed away in September of 2010, at the age of seventy-five.

# PART THREE

"THE TEAM! THE TEAM! THE TEAM!"

# 1969: A Monumental Upset of No. 1 Ohio State

Dan Dierdorf, a blocker's blocker who was inducted into both the College Football Hall of Fame and Pro Football Hall of Fame, said that November 22, 1969, was the greatest day of his life. There was no way Michigan was supposed to beat defending national champion Ohio State on that cool, sunny afternoon in Ann Arbor. The No. 1 Buckeyes had won 22 consecutive games, beaten every opponent that season by at least 27 points, and a *Sports Illustrated* article suggested that perhaps they should play the NFL powerhouse Minnesota Vikings for a challenge.

However, the Wolverines, under first-year coach Bo Schembechler, were on a roll and ranked No. 12. They had gone on the road in their previous two games to beat Illinois, 57–0, and then Iowa, 51–6. They had won four consecutive Big Ten games by a combined score of 178–22.

Then they had what *Ann Arbor News* sports editor Wayne DeNeff, who attended practices during Schembechler's entire career, described as the best week of preparation he'd ever seen. Schembechler left no motivational stone unturned, having bed sheets with "50" inscribed on them hung for players to pass through entering the showers as well as "50" decals stuck on lockers and demonstration team members wearing No. 50—a reminder of Buckeyes coach Woody Hayes going for two points at the end of the 1968 game in Columbus, rubbing salt into the wounds of a 50–14 loss.

"When somebody asked Woody why he went for two," recalled Wolverines offensive guard Reggie McKenzie, a future College Football Hall of Famer, "he said, 'Because I couldn't go for three.' We said, '[Blank] you!' So, we made it a point to remember that. [Team captain and MVP] Jim Mandich promised those seniors that we would beat Ohio State the next year, and we did. There were tears."

Schembechler shoveled snow off the practice field with the freshmen that week, masterfully broke down the tendencies of the Buckeyes' All-America quarterback Rex Kern and safety Jack Tatum during the week, and then sent his team off with fire and brimstone.

Tailback Glenn Doughty recalled the pregame speech:

"Bo said, 'How dare they say this is the Team of the Century? We're the Team of the Century!' Before he could finish, someone shouted, 'Let's go, Bo!' and the place went wild. Guys were throwing chairs and beating lockers down. It was like an earthquake, and we had to leave for our own safety.

"We were David going after Goliath, but not with a rock. We had a nuclear bomb. We were on a mission to kick ass. We were like piranhas, and Ohio State was the little fish. We could not wait to eat those little suckers alive. Psychologists would say we couldn't play on that emotion all day, but it lasted through the entire game and into the parties that night."

Fullback Fritz Seyferth was as much of a "David" as anyone, taking on the most-feared "Goliath" in scarlet and gray. He recalled going against Tatum, nicknamed "The Assassin."

"I was a skinny sophomore and Jack Tatum was my responsibility on the kickoff returns. He was the end man, and I had to kick him out. I can remember vividly blocking him out of the play the first time, and then knocking him out of bounds the second time, and the third time he ran out of bounds. I'm going, 'Whoa' (laughter). I had no business being in the game against Jack Tatum. That's a mismatch if there ever was. Things were just meant to be that game. It went exactly the way you thought it should go.

"What I cherish most is the feeling of getting into the zone or the flow. I can remember taking the field so vividly. It was like your feet didn't touch the ground; everything was so effortless. You just floated down the field."

The Wolverines sprinted down the tunnel of the Big House and proceeded to score 17 unanswered points in a 24–12 victory. It was an ironic scoring run for a 17-point underdog.

"The thing that I hold most dear about that day is that it was about more than just specifically that game," Dierdorf said. "Those of us on that team realize that we

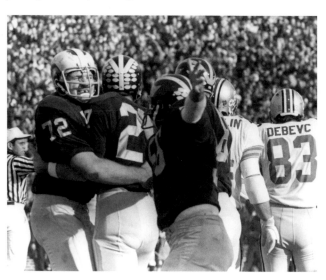

were there at ground zero for the beginning of the modern era of Michigan football.

"That win over Ohio State changed everything, and it announced to the world that the guy with the funny last name, well, there might be more to him than was suspected. It was the

Dan Dierdorf hugs quarterback Don Moorhead with fellow offensive lineman and lifelong friend Dick Caldarazzo approaching to celebrate during the 1969 Ohio State upset.
*Courtesy of Bentley Historical Library, University of Michigan.*

Part Three

beginning of that great run of Bo's, and it changed Michigan football and our stature across the country."

Schembechler won the first of 13 Big Ten titles in his 21 seasons, and the Wolverines made it 21 conference titles in the next 36 years.

"I was just a young whippersnapper then," Schembechler, who was forty in 1969, said in a twentieth-anniversary story in the *Detroit Free Press*. "I was struggling with that team [being 3–2 at midseason]. But when we won, I knew it was big—real big."

Bo's eyes danced at the memory of his signature win.

Cornerback Barry Pierson intercepted three passes and returned a punt 60 yards, to the OSU 3 yard line, to set up the game's final touchdown run by gritty quarterback Don Moorhead.

"The key to football is emotion," Pierson said in that anniversary story. "Everyone played 150 percent for four quarters that day. Bo had us ready to do anything. I never experienced anything else like that day."

Jim Brandstatter, the longtime radio voice of the Wolverines and an offensive tackle on that team, said, "In Michigan history, I don't think there was ever a bigger game played than by Barry Pierson in the Ohio State game of 1969. He played in the backfield with an All-American in Tom Curtis and we had Thom Darden, a very highly regarded sophomore. In the biggest game on the biggest stage, Barry Pierson outdid them all. He didn't have the name recognition or reputation, but he was the best player on the field on that day. Amidst Jack Tatum and Rex Kern and [Buckeyes fullback] Jim Otis and Dan Dierdorf and Jim Mandich and Tom Curtis (who made two interceptions in that game), all those great names and others, Barry Pierson had one of the greatest impacts in Michigan history in that game.

"We were all fired up, that was the thing. You don't pull that kind of upset with one guy having a great game. You do it with all of you having the great game, and all of you being prepared, and all of you on top of your game. And we did that that day, but Barry just had one of those days. Everything slowed down and Barry was in the right place at the right time at every occasion, and when the opportunity came, he took it and exploited it. He didn't shy away from it. We were all in that same mind-set, that we were going to win this game whatever it took. He made the plays, though."

Fullback Garvie Craw scored two touchdowns and ran for 56 yards. Tailback Billy Taylor rushed for 84 yards, and Moorhead ran for 67 yards and passed for 108. All-America tight end Mandich had six catches for 78 yards.

"It was very pure and real," Mandich, who died of cancer in 2011, said in 1989. "I had a lot of emotional games in the pros [four Super Bowls], but what I always come back to in the meanderings of my mind is that game."

It ended with the same kind of off-the-charts emotion that it began with.

"From the beginning to the end of that game," said McKenzie, "that place was the loudest ever. I don't know that anyone ever sat down. It was electric; you could feel it in the air. And after the game, the fans came down and tore down the goal posts.

"If you were there, you will never forget it. Nobody was supposed to beat Ohio State."

Dierdorf said the team partied "well into the night," and they did that together, too.

"You didn't want to be anywhere where you weren't in the company of your teammates," he said. "We were so euphoric about what happened that we went wherever it was as a team. We were all together and in no hurry to separate."

It was that unwavering camaraderie that made them operate so well on a football field.

There was a definite brotherhood about that 1969 Michigan team that was the trailblazer for the greatness that followed.

Dierdorf, a long-time analyst for national network NFL games who began working as the radio analyst for Michigan games in 2014, recalled covering a San Francisco 49ers game when Jim Harbaugh was their coach. They talked about Michigan, and Dierdorf told Harbaugh that the '69 players sometimes felt "self-conscious" about getting too much credit for the success of the Wolverines' modern era.

Dierdorf recalled: "Jim said: 'Don't think that. Don't think that at all. You guys deserve whatever everybody wants to say about you.' But I thought that Jim was no different than I. We both played for Bo and worshipped the ground that he walked on."

Schembechler realized he spoke of the '69 team more than any other he coached. But he told Dierdorf there was a reason for that, and it went far beyond the actual victory itself.

Schembechler told Dierdorf: "The reason is that I didn't recruit a one of you. Not one of you came to Michigan to play for Bo Schembechler. You came to play for somebody else, and this is Bump Elliott's team. The reason that I have always held you guys with such respect and so close to my heart is because you bought into what I was trying to sell you and what I was trying to do. If you wouldn't have, I wouldn't ever have lasted. So I owe the '69 team a debt of gratitude."

Why did those Wolverines buy into such a tough taskmaster, who Dierdorf said was so "unbelievably demanding" that a large number of players quit that first year.

"He was more demanding than anybody we'd ever known," said Dierdorf, "but he did it with a personality. There were times Bo could make us laugh, and he did things that were inherently funny. There's a curious thing that happens when somebody pushes you further than you ever thought possible. You drag through it, kicking and screaming, but when you get to the other side of it, you begrudgingly develop this admiration."

So many monumental upsets are aberrations—unexplainable examples of how on any given day, anything can happen.

That's where this upset was different. The better team—to paraphrase Schembechler's pregame speech—won on that day. Goliath had discovered his long-lost twin brother. "The Big Two and Little Eight" had been created.

In the celebration of the 1969 upset of Ohio State in Ann Arbor, Michigan, assistant coach George Mans is to the direct right of No. 12, wingback James Schmitz. Coach Bo Schembechler is directly behind Mans and being hoisted onto the shoulders of his players. Also expressing great joy are No. 88, All-America tight end Jim Mandich, No. 18, wingback John Gabler, No. 67, offensive guard Joseph Lukz, and to the far right, assistant coach Frank Maloney.
*Courtesy of Bentley Historical Library, University of Michigan.*

# Coach Bo Schembechler

Would the greatness the Michigan football program has realized over the last half century have occurred without Bo Schembechler?

I seriously doubt it.

Now, Wolverine athletic director Don Canham did have another coach in the mix to replace Bump Elliott. Some guy named Joe Paterno, who turned down the first offer. But if it had been anyone else, the last fifty years might have been considerably different on football Saturdays in Ann Arbor.

What Schembechler did is rivaled only by what Fielding H. Yost accomplished in setting the table for the first fifty years of greatness for Michigan. He brought in not only great players but great coaches. And those coaches have been the key to the continued success.

Gary Moeller, his handpicked replacement, was one of the most underrated coaches college football has ever known, recruiting as well as his mentor and moving the offense into a pro-style attack.

Lloyd Carr followed Moeller into the job and maintained the high character of the program while winning a national championship in 1997. Carr also followed Bo into the College Football Hall of Fame.

Bill McCartney, the coach Bo hired straight out of Dearborn (Michigan) Divine Child High, was charismatic and driven. Many speculated he'd be the one to replace Bo, but he would've had to wait too long. He took the job at Colorado, led them to a national championship in 1990, and also is in the College Football Hall of Fame.

Jim Harbaugh, easily the best quarterback Schembechler coached, returned to redirect the Wolverines as a head coach, bringing in the great assistant coaches and talent just like Bo.

So what exactly made Schembechler so special?

I covered his teams as a beat writer at the *Ann Arbor News* and *Detroit Free Press*, and it never ceased to amaze me what an exceptional leader he was. And his greatest gift as that leader was his ability to motivate players like nobody I've been around in more than forty years of covering legendary coaches such as Sparky Anderson, Scotty Bowman, and Chuck Daly.

Anderson and Daly were supreme at getting players to believe in their talents and that they were perhaps even better than they thought. Bowman was the master team builder in terms of knowing what players he could win big with and then putting them in offensive and defensive schemes that absolutely flourished on the ice.

They were all great, but nobody rallied a team to the cause of victory like Schembechler.

I think that's because he didn't have to con players into performing. He made playing for the Wolverines seem like the greatest thing on earth and got them so fired up that they could bust down the locker room door to get to the tunnel. This actually happened before Michigan took the field against Ohio State in 1969 for a monumental upset of a 17-point favorite accomplished in convincing fashion.

He made all the hard work and dedication fun somehow by getting guys who bought into his mantra: "The Team! The Team! The Team!"

"The Team!" speech, recorded in 1983 as he spoke to his squad, is played with an accompanying video at every Michigan sporting event that has a scoreboard with a video screen. Fans stop conversations to listen to it. I've heard it countless times now, and it still captivates me every time.

An edited version of the speech, focusing on its culmination, runs on the video, but here is the complete, unabridged version that takes you into the locker room before that season—which ended with a berth in the Sugar Bowl—with Bo and his boys:

"We want the Big Ten championship, and we're gonna win it as a Team. They can throw out all those great backs, and great quarterbacks, and great defensive players, throughout the country and in this conference, but there's gonna be one Team that's gonna play solely as a Team.

"No man is more important than The Team. No coach is more important than The Team. The Team! The Team! The Team! And if we think that way, all of us, everything that you do, you take into consideration what effect does it have on my Team? Because you can go into professional football, you can go anywhere you want to play after you leave here. You will never play for a Team again. You'll play for a contract. You'll play for this. You'll play for that. You'll play for everything except the team, and think what a great thing it is to be a part of something that is, The Team.

"We're gonna win it. We're gonna win the championship again because we're gonna play as a Team, better than anybody else in this conference, we're gonna play together as a Team. We're gonna believe in each other, we're not gonna criticize each other, we're not gonna talk about each other, we're gonna encourage each other. And when we play as a Team, when the old season is over, you and I know, it's gonna be Michigan again, Michigan!"

A great leader in his realm was captured for Wolverines fans for years to come to hear. It's a goosebumps experience, for sure.

Dan Dierdorf, an All-America offensive tackle in 1970, said Schembechler was a great leader because he was able to develop players with his demanding nature but also laughed with them. And he was a master psychologist.

"We were warming up before a game, and Bo was walking the line," said Dierdorf. "Our opponents are 90 yards down field, and Bo points to them."

Bo: "You see them down there?"

Dan: "Yes, sir, I see them."

Bo: "You know what they are?"

Dan: "No, I don't."

Bo: "They're afraid! And do you know why?"

Dierdorf recalled the veins popping out of Schembechler's neck at that point.

Dan: "No, I don't, Coach."

Bo: "They're afraid because we're MICHIGAN!"

Schembechler then stomped away.

Dierdorf said he looked downfield, the opponents' faces too far away to see clearly, and said to himself, *You know, Coach, I bet you're right.*

He added, "It was just classic."

Dierdorf said Schembechler always drew a crowd when he was in a room because people knew he had something special, entertaining, or both to say.

"He's the most charismatic man I've met in my life," said Dierdorf, who spent over a decade on ABC-TV's *Monday Night Football* team with Frank Gifford and Al Michaels. "And Bo *knew* he was the most charismatic guy there ever was. He used it on a daily basis, and he knew how to use it. He had a real gift."

Fritz Seyferth, a fullback on those first Schembechler teams who made key blocks for tailback Billy Taylor and was later Bo's recruiting coordinator, has studied leadership for a living and made it his calling.

Seyferth focused on dissecting leadership for fourteen years, formed Fritz Seyferth & Associates, and has worked with CEOs of major corporations to improve their businesses with effective leadership models and approaches.

So I could think of no better person to ask about the man's leadership and what put it over the top.

"It was Bo having a singular purpose in life," said Seyferth. "That was to take people places they could never go by themselves, and to realize their potential as a complete person. He wanted not only great football players, but great people who were going to go out into their communities and have a bigger impact on the world than he could ever have himself.

"That's really what drove him—his consistency of purpose. He wanted to, through the game of football, teach people life lessons that they could take into the world."

NFL and other college teams came at Schembechler with grand offers. Seyferth marveled at how his mentor turned down one of those in particular, a ten-year deal with a $1.3 million bonus from Texas A&M "to stay for a $25,000 raise [that put him] at $80,000 (annually)."

Schembechler, fighting back emotion at the January 15, 1982, press conference to announce his decision, said, "I came to the conclusion that there are things that are more important to me, and one of them's Michigan! With that in mind, I'm staying where I belong, right here."

Seyferth fully understood why Bo turned down millions: "It was because he had a calling that he felt was much more important than the money. He couldn't walk away from the character of the people and what the institution represented. He was a pretty wise man."

He added that players didn't necessarily "buy into" Schembechler's methods while playing for him. But they followed him because of something they strongly sensed about the man and how he related to them.

"He had an unconditional love for them," said Seyferth. "Whenever you went into his office, he demonstrated that he loved you … unless you were not committed to the team. If you were a selfish player or a 'me' player or wanted more than you rightly deserved, he would try to straighten you out if he could. But he might drive you off the team, too."

That brought to mind a situation after the 1984 season, when Michigan went 6–6, and I asked Schembechler what had gone wrong. He told me he recruited three players who weren't "Michigan Men," but he believed the hundred-plus others could convert them into being team players. He told me he was wrong and had to get rid of those players, who had begun taking others the wrong way.

"That is exactly what happened," said Seyferth. "I can remember that so vividly."

Bo said he had to recruit his entire team all over again, selling them on the Michigan way. He got quick results, too. The Wolverines, after beating Nebraska in the Fiesta Bowl to cap the 1985 season, finished No. 2 in the Associated Press poll for Bo's highest finish.

That "unconditional love," Seyferth said, was the most important element to Schembechler's ability to lead.

"Absolutely," said Seyferth. "That's absolutely what it was. You knew he wasn't there for himself or a win for his record. He was there to develop people. He was able to motivate people to do the right thing.

"I had wondered if there was a way you could systematize winning, and is there a recipe to success? And there is, and Bo lived it. There are a few leaders who were born that way. It's just in their DNA to do the right thing, and Bo was one of them.

"The keys to his leadership was a purpose that's in service of others before yourself. That's deeply meaningful to the people you're working with. That's the first one. The second one is the guiding principle of love, that you love the people you're doing it for and doing it with. Next is trust, and we trusted Bo. You knew what he said was the way it was going to be. He didn't flip-flop. He did what he said he was going to do and expected you to do what you said you were going to do."

Seyferth asked Bo how he had a knack for doing the right thing at the right time.

"And he said, 'I didn't. But I knew if I didn't act like I knew, the team wouldn't follow me. If they followed me, I knew they'd win.'

Bo Schembechler coaching portrait.
*Courtesy of Bentley Historical Library, University of Michigan.*

"We are all richer and blessed to have been in his presence, and so much wiser for it."

Seyferth is one of those who Schembechler helped accomplish more than he could have done himself, and his company's mission is an example of that, too.

"The difference we make in people's lives at home and in their offices is astounding," said Seyferth.

Glenn Edward "Shemy" Schembechler III said his father inspired his players by setting a great example and then noted what he saw as the root of his leadership greatness.

"It was because he was completely unselfish," said Shemy. "He always looked out for others' best interests. One of the things that gets missed in 'The Team! The Team! The Team!' speech is the one sentence: 'No coach is more important than The Team.' And he lived that. He basically took his own self-interest and made it subservient to the overall cause.

"People need to remember that now. We're in a world now where egotism has run rampant, and people miss the boat in regard to Bo—and this is how Woody Hayes trained him—but Woody was one of the most unselfish people ever."

Bo's father was known as Shem, and his son became Shemy, who decided that his son will also be known as Bo.

"His sisters, Virginia and Marge, both called my dad Bo-Bo because they couldn't say brother," said Shemy. "It was predetermined that I would call our son Bo. I'm not going to break the chain. This is fourth generation here, and we want to preserve that legacy as best we can.

"We're not going to steer Bo into football or coaching, but there's a stronger legacy behind his name, and what it means to have character and honesty and integrity. It's not so much about vocation or what you do every day. It's about who you are."

Shemy was an NFL scout for 15 seasons with the Kansas City Chiefs, Chicago Bears, and Washington Redskins and served as a consultant to the Seattle Seahawks for one year before launching GES Advisory Company in 2015. He aims to "take the NFL scouting mode to high school football" and thoroughly evaluate talent at all levels before recommending them as a prospect in the NAIA or the three divisions of NCAA football. He does that through evaluation, coaching, networking, and a full report for parents and players who become clients.

One important reason for changing his professional route was to be home more with Bo, who was born February 19, 2009. He's the only child of Shemy and his wife, Megan, who make their home in Columbus, Ohio. That should bring a chuckle from Michigan fans, but Shemy remains maize and blue through and through in the land of scarlet and gray.

Shemy and Bo Schembechler share a moment together. Shemy was a scout for the Washington Redskins and his father was retired as Michigan's winningest football coach at the time of this photo.
*Photo Courtesy of Shemy Schembechler.*

His father's integrity was inspired by his grandfather, and Shemy shared the story that capsulizes that so well.

"It's one of the greatest stories of all time," said Shemy, recalling the time his grandfather was preparing for the civil service test required prior to interviewing for the fire chief position in Barberton, Ohio.

"They had gotten a copy of the test that his competitor for the job already had," Shemy continued. "But he said, 'I'm going to get this job legitimately if I get it.' He wouldn't take the copy of the test. Obviously, the other guy got the job and lied through his teeth about taking it legitimately.

"So, the day after he took the job, Grandpa Shemy went into his office and confronted him. He said, 'I know how you got this job, and I will never work one day for you.' Grandpa hung up a twenty-five-year career as a fireman to form his own business, and become a fire inspector and an electrician, and did that until the day he died."

Shem died of a heart attack while Bo was on Hayes's coaching staff at Ohio State.

Shemy recalled a story of how Hayes, hated by many Wolverines fans for his earlier dominance of Michigan and intimidating manner, created a fund by selling brand new cars given to him annually by a Columbus car dealer to help OSU students who could not pay their tuition. Shemy said that research was done to determine Hayes paid for the education of 258 students.

"I just think that if Bo were here today," said his son, "to look back on his life, he would be saying, 'I was just doing what I was trained to do.' You take Betty Schembechler, his mother, who is exactly who he got his personality from, and his father and Woody, and you put those three people together and those were the ones who formed his character and who he was. He would want to pay reverence to those people.

"Grandma could give him [crap] and he'd listen."

Shemy chuckled at that memory.

After Michigan won that Fiesta Bowl to finish No. 2, I called Bo at the team hotel. Betty picked up the phone, and we had an animated conversation. She promised to have Bo call when he returned, and he did. Without Betty, there probably was no way Bo would've called me. But he did and was in such a great mood that day, so happy to be so close to the top after that one season that was his rock-bottom at Michigan.

"Grandpa Shemy was a quiet man," said Shemy. "He wasn't very rambunctious, but the cantankerousness, that came from Betty. She took my dad and his older sisters to Cleveland Indians games on Sundays and loved sports."

Shemy said his mother, Millie, took lessons from Betty. It was generally agreed upon that they were the only two people on the planet who could get their way with Bo.

Bo Schembechler poses with wife Millie and son Shemy.
*Courtesy of Bentley Historical Library, University of Michigan.*

After Millie died of cancer in 1992, Shemy joined Gary Moeller's staff as the assistant recruiting coordinator and had an office directly across the hall from his father in Schembechler Hall, which was originally called the Center of Champions because Bo didn't want it named for him.

"I got to spend every single day with him," said Shemy. "We did a lot of catching up, and it was the most special period of time. And when he died, I knew I would never forget those two years with him at Michigan. It was huge.

"You know, all we can do is live out their legacy, and do what they would've done. You have to plot your own course. But it's that trust, honesty and love that you have for others, that came from my parents, and transcends all the things we should be as men."

His father died of heart failure on November 17, 2006, on the eve of the show-down between No. 1 Ohio State and No. 2 Michigan in Columbus, a game the Buckeyes won, 42–39. It was difficult focusing on football after the loss of Schem-bechler, who was honored with a moment of silence on game day at Ohio Stadium.

The silence was broken with a reading that concluded:

"Michigan has lost a coach and patriarch. The Big Ten has lost a legend and icon. Ohio State has lost an alumnus and friend. The Schembechler family has lost a beloved father, grandfather, and husband.

"Bo made the game of football better in every way. Our thoughts and prayers are with his family and everyone who mourns his passing."

He was inspiring the Wolverines right up to the day before he died when he addressed the team in Ann Arbor.

Coach Carr told the 15,000-plus who showed up to celebrate his life at Michigan Stadium in the days ahead: "He told our team, 'You're going to go out and do a lot of great things in your life, but you are never going to have the great experiences you've had at Michigan.'"

Jim Brandstatter played on those first Schembechler teams, backing up Dierdorf before getting his chance to start in 1971. He then covered Bo as a broadcaster before becoming the radio voice of the Wolverines and hosting the coach's TV show longer than anyone else.

What's his most lasting memory of Schembechler and his leadership as a player?

"There are millions of them," said Brandstatter, chuckling. "He pushed us as hard as we could be pushed, and some of us liked playing for him because he was demanding and tough, and he did push us further than we could go, and yet we went there and we ultimately won, and after we graduated and we realized there was a method to his madness, he became one of our dearest friends and one of the people we admired most because we appreciated that he had pushed us so hard to get the most out of us. But we couldn't appreciate it until we were gone."

Brandstatter then saw Schembechler take that same approach with the reporters who covered him:

"He tested you and he pushed you, and if you gave in and just kind of rolled over to play dead, you got nothing. But if you stayed at it and didn't go away, he respected that and gave you a lot of good information. Bo appreciated your work ethic and your work."

Which was exactly what I encountered—to a pretty extreme level both good and bad—in covering Bo and his team from 1983 through 1989, when he retired before briefly staying on as Michigan's athletic director.

Schembechler did his best to ignore me at first. That was actually better than what followed. He called *Ann Arbor News* editor-in-chief Brian Malone to ask that he either fire me or take me off the Michigan football beat.

Malone asked Bo why he wanted me removed, and he told my editor that I was ruining his recruiting efforts by publicizing their every move with the country's top players. Malone asked him if my reports were accurate, and Bo said they were. Bo noted a few other stories that I wrote that he didn't care for, and again Malone asked the same question. "Yes," Bo told him, "they were accurate."

"Steve will be covering your football team as long as I am the editor of the *Ann Arbor News*," Malone told Bo, who harrumphed and hung up the phone.

Bo was the supreme dictator of almost anything he chose to claim in Ann Arbor, and so this was not as easy as an editor citing journalistic ethics and wishing some civic leader "good day" after stating his case. Malone stood by me, though.

Still, there was one more major hurdle that I had to clear with Bo, and it had to do with the recruitment of Andre Rison, the Flint Northwestern star who would go on to set Michigan State's career receiving yardage record that stood for nearly a quarter-century. He would become an All-American and the first-round pick of the Indianapolis Colts before tearing up the NFL.

Bo wanted him badly, but Rison committed to Michigan State coach George Perles, and Bo had a theory as to why.

"*You* COST ME Andre Rison, damn it!" Bo shouted at me on a phone call one day in 1985.

Bo said my story in which Ann Arbor Pioneer High receiver Cedric Gordon said he would commit to Michigan if he met academic requirements had caused problems with Rison. Bo said Rison was upset because Bo had promised that he would not recruit another receiver in the state, and Bo then told me on the phone that there was no way he was going to sign Gordon.

I told Bo that after Gordon and his coach, Chuck Lori, confirmed for me that his intentions were Michigan if his grades and test scores were in line, I called him and Seyferth to ask if Gordon were being recruited in light of his questionable academic situation. This can be a slippery slope for reporters and coaches because

NCAA rules don't allow them to discuss recruits with the media. But I wanted to do my due diligence and provide both sides of the story.

Neither Bo nor Seyferth would comment about Gordon, either on or off the record.

"Bo," I said, "it has to be a two-way street between us if you want stories to include your point of view."

He shot back: "It's NOT going to be any *damned* two-way street. Got it?"

Bo liked to punctuate statements with "Got it?" when he was on a roll.

"Hey," Bo continued, "I've got to know one thing from you."

He paused for effect.

"I've got to know if you're *for* me or *against* me!"

I told Bo that I could be neither.

"I can't be your public relations man," I said. "And I won't be a hatchet man, looking to cut you down. All I can be is fair."

It was odd that Bo had no response to my explanation.

"Goodbye," he said before hanging up the phone.

But something struck a chord with Bo during that conversation, and he began to warm up to having me around. Then he actually began to *like* having me on the beat. Bo started letting me into occasional practices, was critical in helping me break a few stories, and showed me another side that I never figured I would see.

I guess he just wanted to put me up against the wall and see how I would respond.

Everything was a test with Bo. He challenged everybody because he was that confident in who he was and what he demanded.

The access never was better than after his final game against Ohio State, when I got to share in the overflowing emotions of the coach and his team after that victory.

As we all ran through the tunnel after the game, Michigan equipment manager Jon Falk told me to wait by a locker room door.

Everyone else hurried to the news conference, but I waited there for Falk to open the door. I got to be a fly on the wall as Schembechler stood on a stool in the center of the room and congratulated his players on winning the championship and Rose Bowl berth.

Then he led them in a singing of "The Victors," all thrusting long-stemmed roses high as they punctuated the song lyrics: "Hail! Hail to Michigan, the champions of the West!"

What a way to go out.

Schembechler won 13 Big Ten titles and a school-record 194 games among his 234 as a college head coach, first at his alma mater, Miami of Ohio. He coached great players such as Desmond Howard, Anthony Carter, Rick Leach, Dan Dierdorf, Rob Lytle, Steve Everitt, Jamie Morris, Jumbo Elliott, and Jim Harbaugh.

He sent players to not only the NFL, but to law school, medical school, and the coaching ranks. And most importantly, he showed them that they needed to build families as strong as the teams they played on.

Bo also was close friends with President Gerald R. Ford, who was the center on Michigan's 1932 and 1933 national championship teams. Ford attended Wolverine football practices and kicked off his 1976 election campaign on campus.

Gerald R. Ford posing to snap the football as a Michigan Wolverine. Ford, the 38th President of the US, was a member of the 1932 and 1933 national championship teams and MVP as a center in 1934.
*Photo Courtesy of Gerald R. Ford Presidential Library.*

The Gerald R. Ford Presidential Library and Museum dedicated a story to the life and career of Schembechler and his relationship with the president in its archives:

Former US President Gerald Ford, the Wolverines' football MVP in 1934, poses at practice on November 10, 1982, with three-time All-America wide receiver Anthony Carter (center) and Wolverines coach Bo Schembechler (right), his good friend.
*Photo Courtesy of Gerald R. Ford Presidential Library.*

"Later in life Bo would become more politically active, often conversing with Ford on the political development of the day. Ford appointed Bo to be one of the pallbearers at his funeral, but Schembechler's death preceded Ford's by a little more than a month. At Ford's funeral a Michigan blanket was placed in the pew to honor Bo Schembechler."

President Ford issued this statement when Schembechler died at the age of seventy-seven:

"Bo Schembechler was an outstanding citizen in every respect. He was a dear friend of ours and will be greatly missed by his numerous friends. It is a great loss to the University of Michigan in particular and football in general.

"Betty and I send our deepest condolences, thoughts, and prayers to Bo's wife Cathy [whom he married in 1993] and their family."

There is only one statue across the vast athletic campus and facilities at Michigan, and it comes as no surprise that it is of the football coach who showed the way. It's a larger-than-life likeness in bronze, sculpted by J. Brett Grill and unveiled in 2014 at the entrance to Schembechler Hall, home to the Wolverines football program.

Bo is captured moving forward, headset in hand, baseball cap and sunglasses contributing to the iconic look. He's wearing a coaching jacket and football cleats, and you almost feel like it's a brisk fall afternoon when you see his likeness there.

Before the opening game of the 2017 season, someone placed three red roses in his clenched right fist, symbolism for what was always his ultimate quest: a Big Ten championship and a trip to the Rose Bowl.

Fans stop at all times of the day and night to pose with the Bo statue for a photo, and I even caught a handful of skateboarders shooting a video with Bo as their background. Sometimes I look up at it and chuckle, maybe even say something to the statue, like it is really Bo frozen there forever in time.

And I wonder what Michigan football would've been like without Schembechler, and I can't even imagine it.

# The Block M:
# Michigan's Outstanding Offensive Line Tradition

The Block M has been a powerful movement.

There are few, if any, position groups at schools across the nation that have experienced the productivity and accolades bestowed upon the University of Michigan offensive linemen over the last half century.

They blocked for 21 Big Ten championship teams, 1969 to 2017, and produced 42 selections in those 49 seasons that were named first team All-America or taken in the first round of the NFL Draft. Players earning both distinctions were not counted twice in the total.

Seven of those blocking tackles, guards, centers, and tight ends were two-time All-Americans: Mark Donahue (1976–77), John "Jumbo" Elliott (1986–87), Greg Skrepenak (1990–91), Steve Hutchinson (1999–2000), Jake Long (2006–07), Taylor Lewan (2012–13), and Jake Butt (2015–16).

Nine of them were first-round selections: Paul Seymour (1972), Mike Kenn (1978), Jon Giesler (1979), Steve Everitt (1993), Trezelle "Tree" Jenkins (1995), Jeff Backus (2001), Hutchinson (2001), Long (2008), and Lewan (2014). They were among the sixty-three Wolverine blockers drafted in that 49-season span.

"We all take an unbelievable amount of pride in that," said Jon Jansen, an All-America right tackle in 1998. "I was a huge fan of Michigan football growing up and knew of Dierdorf and Bubba Paris (1981) and all those guys who came before us and started this great tradition—guys like [Joe] Cocozzo (1992

All-American), Everitt, and [Doug] Skene (1992 first team All-Big Ten), who came before us.

"And you hear the stories about not only what they did on the field but off the field, and in practices and workouts. To be a part of that unit, do what I did, and say I was a Michigan offensive lineman was a huge honor for me."

Tight end Jim Mandich (1969), tackle Dan Dierdorf (1970), and guard Reggie McKenzie (1971) are the three "Block M" members since Coach Bo Schembechler's arrival to be elected to the College Football Hall of Fame. Ironically, all three were second-round draft picks who went on to highly successful NFL careers as well.

They were the modern era trailblazers.

Michigan has had an excellence in offensive linemen dating all the way back to center William Cunningham, the school's very first All-American in 1898. Cunningham was selected on the recommendation of legendary University of Chicago coach Amos Alonzo Stagg for his performance in the Wolverines' win over his team that season and went on to become a medical missionary in China in a time that predated the NFL.

Reggie McKenzie, one of the top pulling guards the college game has ever seen, turns the corner on a blocking assignment.
*Courtesy of Bentley Historical Library, University of Michigan.*

However, the dominance of the "Block M" rose to another level when Schembechler, an offensive lineman for Sid Gillman and Woody Hayes at Miami of Ohio, came to Ann Arbor in 1969.

McKenzie, a 6-foot-4, 232-pound search-and-destroy pulling guard, said Schembechler was the one who prepared him for the rigors of the NFL:

"He said, 'Do it right every time, all the time and the first time.' He was the one who really prepared me both physically and mentally to go on and play on Sundays, and take that same attitude out in life."

Schembechler brought along with him another Miami product, Jerry Hanlon, a fiery and knowledgeable offensive line coach who demanded and received excellence on the field.

"You go back to 1969," said Michigan quarterback legend Rick Leach, "when Michigan had one of the greatest upsets in the history of football against Ohio State. You go back to those days with the Dan Dierdorfs, Reggie McKenzies, and Paul Seymours.

"The guys that I played with, we had All-Americans. Mike Kenn didn't get a lot of publicity in college but was the (No. 13 overall) first-round pick of the Atlanta Falcons. John Wangler had a great offensive line. Jim Harbaugh had a great offensive line."

Leach, who had a then NCAA-record 82 touchdowns passing and running during his career in the mid-1970s, was making the point that while quarterbacks get the glory, they get nowhere without quality blocking.

What twenty of those All-America blockers have in common is Hanlon. He was a Michigan assistant from 1969 to 1991 and focused on the program's mammoth linemen with the exception of a half dozen seasons late in his tenure as the quarterbacks coach.

"Jerry Hanlon deserves to be recognized as one of the greatest teachers of offensive line play that ever walked on a football field," said Dierdorf. "But also, don't forget that Jerry wore a lot of different hats. Jerry and Bo had a 'good cop-bad cop' thing going. We'd be so furious with Bo about how he was pushing us, but Jerry would be the guy who would say, 'Stick with me. We'll get through this.'"

Dierdorf said Schembechler spent his time with the quarterbacks in practice. Hanlon had complete control in regard to the linemen.

Everitt, one of his most efficient and punishing blockers, said that having played for Hanlon gave him instant credibility in the NFL.

"I had a workout with the [Los Angeles] Rams and Jim Hanifan before my last season in the NFL," said Everitt. "Hanifan was another O-line guru I got to play for, and he put me through this workout and started laughing halfway through it and said, 'Why are we even doing this? Your technique is perfect. Jerry Hanlon was your damn coach!'"

Hanifan got his first taste of a Hanlon product when he began coaching Dierdorf for the St. Louis Cardinals. Dierdorf recalled Hanifan, running backs coach Joe Gibbs, and head coach Don Coryell approaching him following a blocking drill.

Dierdorf recalled: "They said: 'Who taught you to do this?' And then I made the biggest mistake of my professional football career. I told them it was this little Irishman in Ann Arbor named Jerry Hanlon. Hanifan went to Ann Arbor to learn how Jerry did it, and he came back to St. Louis with the cages and the boards, and my fellow linemen didn't talk to me for six months.

"Hanlon had these metal frames that were higher in the back than they were in the front, and then he put a two-by-four board on the ground. And he put a live defensive lineman in front of you, straddling that board, and you had to block him.

"If you came out high, you hit your head on the metal crossbar. And if you got your feet too narrow, you would step on the board and fall flat on your face. Jerry invented that cage, and every Michigan offensive lineman Jerry reared came out of that chute thousands of times. Everything was completely precise: your right foot replaced your right hand and everything was symmetrical. As Bo would say, 'It was about keeping the long axis of your body perpendicular to the goal line.' Every part of your body went north and south. There was no east and west.

"The narrower your feet get, the less power you have, and so you learn to keep your feet spread at shoulder-width. And you've got to come out low and get under the defensive lineman's pad level because if you came out high, you got KO'd by that iron crossbar above you. It was a tremendous teaching tool."

Dierdorf said that approach wouldn't work today because blocking is done much higher with more hand work.

Hanlon never liked taking bows when the performances of his pupils were noted. He preferred to heap the praise back onto his players.

"Well, I don't know how much I had to do with it," said Hanlon, chuckling. "But I do know that I'm really proud of all the guys I coached who went on to play pro football. But, I'll tell you this, I'm just as proud of those who went on to (outstanding careers outside of athletics)."

Hanlon's players would do anything for him.

Part Three

"You have coaches that you play for," said Everitt, "and you have coaches that you would go out and kill for. I would have gone out there and killed, done anything, for Coach Hanlon. He came here from the get-go with Bo, and you knew he'd been through all those wars with Bo.

"I felt lucky to have played for Bo for two years, and I felt lucky to get coached by Coach Hanlon. I mean, he's the guru of O-line coaches. I was so lucky with the coaches I had. That's why I went to Michigan."

The Block M caught Everitt's eye when he was a freshman at Miami Southridge High. His beloved Miami Hurricanes, ranked No. 1, went into Ann Arbor under Jimmy Johnson and were beaten, 22–14, by the Wolverines.

"Miami had just won the national championship," said Everitt, "and Michigan just kicked Miami's ass. I was almost scared of the Michigan offensive line from watching that game on TV. Once Michigan started recruiting me, it clicked that I

Steve Everitt snaps the ball to Michigan quarterback Elvis Grbac against Iowa in 1992. The dominating center was a first-round draft pick of the Cleveland Browns the following April. *AP Photo/Bill Waugh.*

had a chance to go there. I wanted to be a part of that. And once I talked to Bo, it was a done deal. Bo had tradition. I still live and die for Michigan.

"When you think linemen, you think of Michigan. You think of Jake Long and Dan Dierdorf. I could name twenty guys right now, and each one better than the last. And just to have been able to be a part of that makes me proud, just to be mentioned with some of those guys."

Jon Jansen, the Big Ten's Offensive Lineman of the Year in 1998, said that aura of toughness also is what attracted him.

"One of the reasons I came to Michigan was because of what Les Miles told me when he sat me down in a room," said Jansen, who switched from tight end to tackle as a redshirt freshman and set a record for Wolverines O-linemen with 50 consecutive starts. "He talked about how he would teach us to play football.

"I'm an aggressive individual when I'm on the football field, and I loved the fact that he brought so much emotion and passion to the offensive linemen at Michigan. He said, 'We're going to teach you how to punch and knock the air out of another man's chest!' I'm sitting there and saying, 'Lets go!'"

Toughness was central to their success.

"Everitt played with a broken jaw!" said Jansen. "He's laying on the ground spitting blood and [after missing just one start] he comes right back. I'm a freshman in high school [in Clawson, Michigan] and I'm thinking to myself, 'I want to be a part of that.' I had a chance to play more games on the offensive line at Michigan than anyone until Mason Cole—and I love that Mason broke that record—and I still want another start.

"We had so many tough-ass guys, and I wanted to come here and be that guy. And then guys like Jake Long wanted to be like us. We had to hear about Everitt and Cocozzo and Skrepenak, and you love the fact that you're a part of that history. But I said, 'Damn it! I want them to hear about Jansen, Backus, and Hutchinson.' What I tell our linemen today is, 'You've got to go out there and make them talk about you guys.' You want to be that dominant, physical player until the whistle blows."

Jansen, who played 10 of his 11 NFL seasons for the Washington Redskins and made the last of 125 starts for the Detroit Lions, has worked for the Big Ten Network and is part of the Michigan radio network's game day shows, and has even subbed for Dierdorf as the analyst for several games. That allows him to be around the current Wolverines on a regular basis.

He has become friends with Everitt, who recently became friends with John Arbeznik, a captain for Schembechler in 1979 who was an all-conference guard.

Part Three

They are part of the Block M Brotherhood, and they're all proud and remain supportive of Hanlon. They honored him and the late Tirrel Burton, Hanlon's college teammate and a longtime Wolverines running backs coach, at a get-together prior to a game in 2017, when Harbaugh brought back Hanlon as an honorary captain. More than 400 turned out.

Hanlon had recruited many of them, and he knew what he was looking for out of high school players.

"In order to have a really good offensive line," Hanlon said, "you have to have good kids. I think that's the number one thing. While many of them didn't have all the physical talents that you would want to have to be a pro football player, they certainly did have the attributes that you wanted to be a winner, and that's what we looked for.

"I've been really fortunate to have great kids, and you get guys like Dierdorf and Kenn and Giesler and all those guys who went on to make a pretty good living in pro football."

Hanlon played for legendary Notre Dame coach Ara Parseghian at Miami, and said something that Parseghian said at the team banquet after his senior season made an impact.

"Ara made a statement that he thought I was going to become a pretty good football coach," said Hanlon, who began learning about offensive line play as a high school coach. He began refining his approach to the position group as Schembechler's offensive line coach at Miami.

Hanlon learned that character was an absolute necessity before searching for the physical skills.

"If that fit with their size, their strength, their agility, their speed and all the other things," said Hanlon, "then it really all came together."

Hanlon taught them well once they arrived in Ann Arbor.

"The idea was to teach the kids the basic techniques to be successful," said Hanlon. "If you're supposed to knock somebody off the line a couple of yards, then I wanted to teach you how to do it. If I wanted to pull this guy and have him pick up a linebacker scraping, I wanted to do that. If I wanted to teach him how to trap, I wanted to do the basic techniques to take a good inside-out course and make sure I got their head where it needed to be to block the opponent.

"If you teach those and they learn them, you will be able to run the football. And if you run the football, you are going to win. It's as simple as that. Now, you also have to learn other things. You have to learn to protect the passer in the proper sets, how to keep your shoulder square to the line of scrimmage, and all those things. But the fact still remains that if you can't teach the basic techniques, you are not going to be successful."

Dierdorf said the high-volume repetition of the proper technique became engrained with "muscle memory" and fine-tuned blockers rolled out of Ann Arbor like monster trucks off an assembly line.

He noted that mastering the drive block was at the core of the success.

"We didn't spend much time on pass-blocking because the only passes we threw were off play-action [fakes]," said Dierdorf. "We didn't do much in the way of conventional, drop-back passing. Everything involved us coming off the line of scrimmage, and coming off low with a good base.

"Jerry taught all of us to be technicians, and he demanded it. Bo called me into his office after I had been drafted by the Cardinals, and said, 'You're about to go play pro football, and you might have a coach who will tell you what you can and cannot do. But I just want to tell you one thing: You're the best run-blocker in the NFL and you're not even there yet.' That's because Jerry taught me to come off the ball low."

Everitt said: "Jerry was mostly coaching the tackles and tight ends in my senior year, but Les Miles was coaching [the guards and centers]. I don't think you could've had two better offensive line coaches than Les Miles and Jerry Hanlon."

Miles played for Hanlon before becoming part of the coaching staff and went on to great success as the head coach at Oklahoma State and LSU, where he won the national championship in 2007.

Jansen noted that Miles and others continued producing high-caliber linemen after Hanlon retired:

"There were even guys drafted in the later rounds who had substantial careers because of the way we were prepared at Michigan. That goes to guys like Jerry Hanlon, Les Miles, Mike DeBord, and Terry Malone—guys I knew as offensive line coaches."

Hanlon had a gruff exterior and his face would turn beet red when he barked instructions on the practice field, but he also had a heart of gold, and it didn't take his players long to realize that.

The longtime coach said, "I had a few of my players say, 'I'm not so sure I want to be around you very long.'"

He chuckled at the recollection and continued, saying, "But I had so many of them come back and say, 'I didn't know if I wanted to play for you. But I'm surely glad I did.'"

Part Three

Jack Miller, the starting center for Brady Hoke in 2014, wasn't even born when Hanlon coached. Still, he felt a connection to the man who continues nurturing the program's players and coaches. Hanlon still comes on Mondays to review game videotape and writes an annual letter of inspiration given to each player during Ohio State weeks. He still appears on the Michigan radio network's pregame show and was a radio analyst for a number of years after retiring as a coach.

"I got to know Coach Hanlon fairly well because he was around a lot," said Miller. "I spent a lot of time with him this summer at a golf outing. He made those guys and started the tradition of the offensive line at Michigan.

"He's got a big personality for a little guy, and he grabs your attention. He's also a very charming guy, and when he takes command of the room, you heard the message, and you got what he was saying. He's a tough guy and built on discipline and toughness and doing things the right way."

The fact that Hanlon has been able to connect with virtually every offensive lineman since 1969 is central to the generational Block M Brotherhood.

"Give credit to the O-line coaches who have been here after him," said Miller. "They still wanted him to share and be a part. That's what makes Michigan special, and not just from the offensive line perspective. We embrace traditions. We embrace the past, and we build on that. And Jerry was the foundation for that unit and what we now know as one of the better position traditions in college football."

Miller said that Dave Molk, the 2011 Rimington Trophy winner as the nation's top center, "took me under his wing" to show the way.

But he also got sound advice from Long—one of only six offensive linemen drafted No. 1 overall since the NFL began selecting college players in 1936—and the current Michigan radio broadcast tandem of Dierdorf and Jim Brandstatter, who backed up Dierdorf before starting as a senior in 1971. Hutchinson also helped connect Miller to Michigan's tradition.

"Those guys really put their stamp on the college game, Michigan and the NFL," said Miller. "They are legendary guys who you learn about and end up looking up to."

Mason Cole, who tied a school record with 51 consecutive starts at center and left tackle from 2014 to '17, is the only true freshman offensive lineman to start the opening game for the Wolverines.

"I can't imagine another place where it's like it is here," said Cole. "The type of connections we have with former offensive linemen here are incredible. When you've got guys like Jake Long, Steve Everitt, and Steve Hutchinson and on down the list, guys we didn't play with who have been out of Michigan a long time now, they come back and reach out.

"The brotherhood that Michigan brings and builds is special. I still talk to [former teammates] Graham Glasgow, Jack Miller, Kyle Kalis, and Erik Magnuson all the time. But it's not just the guys you played with. It's the guys who played before you and after you."

Cole grew close to Everitt, now an artist living in the Florida Keys.

"I don't know if there are a lot of places where guys just come back for a lifetime," said Cole. "I mean, Everitt will come back for a game every year until he goes. But it's the same with everyone.

"You come to Michigan, and it's a family here. You come here and you join a really incredible family."

On the day after the 2016 Orange Bowl, Everitt brought a catch of blue crabs from his home to the team hotel. He had a feast with Cole and his family.

That get-together exemplified just how much of a family Michigan offensive lineman have become over a half-century. It begins with a commonality possessed by a group that doesn't care about the spotlight and doesn't mind doing the dirty work for the good of the team.

"The offensive line, by nature, has a lot of guys who personality-wise are the same and character-wise are the same," said Miller. "You get a lot of guys with the same mindset—tough, gritty guys. There are never prima donnas up front. They are not looking for credit. They are guys who clock-in, do their jobs, and clock-out. And they find a brotherhood in that.

"I think what makes Michigan so unique is the expectation on the offensive line. There is not another position on the field, offensively or defensively, that so much is expected of. We felt it from the coaches, the media and the fan base. Historically, the offensive line play at Michigan has had some great, great lines and offensive linemen. It starts up front and it always does. You win and lose based on the front unit and it brings guys together and creates a special bond, our brotherhood. It's created a culture that you love to play in. It's, 'Hey, it's on us.'"

The "Block M" is accountable, formidable, and unbreakable.

## 1973: Tie With Ohio State Broke Hearts, Broke Ground

Ties generally become forgotten games. Nobody wins. Nobody loses. And nobody remembers much about those contests.

Then there was the 10–10 tie between No. 1 Ohio State and No. 4 Michigan on November 24, 1973.

The Big Ten Network made a documentary about it. It was a great game. It had drama. And because the conference's athletic directors had to vote on which team would play in the Rose Bowl, it made history with the politics involved and ramifications that resulted. The Big Ten lifted its ban on sending more than one team to a bowl game as a result of such a deserving Michigan team staying home with a 10–0–1 record.

Both teams were undefeated entering the regular-season finale, and ABC-TV broadcaster Chris Schenkel proclaimed: "They meet for the Big Ten championship and possibly the national championship."

The Buckeyes, led by offensive guard John Hicks, the runner-up in Heisman Trophy voting, ran out of the tunnel straight for the M Club banner that the Wolverines traditionally run beneath at midfield en route to taking their sideline before games. They pulled it to the ground, the whole team en masse, before it was recovered and put back in place.

The Michigan players eventually charged out under it, jumping and slapping the banner as they passed. Emotions, rated on a scale of 1 to 10, were an 11.

Defenses dominated play, but Ohio State took a 10–0 lead in the final minute of the first half on a 5-yard run by fullback Pete Johnson. The Wolverines didn't get on the scoreboard until the first minute of the fourth quarter, when Mike Lantry kicked a 30-yard field goal.

"I kicked it right down the middle and it felt good," said Lantry. "We had regrouped, and I felt that put us in a good position."

Michigan quarterback Dennis Franklin connected with tight end Paul Seal for 27 yards to spark the game-tying touchdown drive. Coach Bo Schembechler, faced with 4th-and-inches at the 10 yard line, decided to put it all on the line. Franklin faked a handoff to fullback Ed Shuttlesworth and sprinted to his right to slice through the defense basically untouched for a touchdown.

The NCAA-record crowd of 105,223 in the Big House exploded in celebration as Franklin pranced in the end zone, the ball in his right hand extended high. It was 10-all with 9:32 remaining.

Lantry, nicknamed "Super Toe," got two chances to win the game, but the left-footed kicker's 58-yard attempt—a nearly unheard of distance in that era—was pushed barely wide left.

"It would've been good from sixty yards," Lantry recalled for us. "It had the distance and the wind was swirling, and it was swirling in that direction. But once that wind gets captured, it's kind of mixing bowl effect. And from that far out, the goal posts are pretty small. I wasn't compensating enough for the wind, but I hit it really good and it was in, in and tailed right at the end. People say it was six inches wide."

Both teams lost their starting quarterbacks to injuries late in the game, and Michigan defensive back Tom Drake jumped a route to intercept Greg Hare, who stepped in for Cornelius Greene.

That possession resulted in one more chance for Lantry with 28 seconds remaining, but he was wide right from 44 yards. Buckeyes linebacker Randy Gradishar jumped on the back of lineman Nick Buonamici and tried in vain to block the kick but was a distraction.

"Something happened there that I wasn't used to seeing," said Lantry, "but that didn't have anything to do with how the kick went. I thought someone was going to throw a flag, but they didn't.

"I overcompensated [this time] for the wind and it tailed away from the right upright. I drove it a little harder, and instead of getting sucked in, it tailed even more so. It was a great hold and a great snap. But I didn't hit it the way I wanted, and had the distance on that one, too. I wasn't trying to rush it, but just do what I'd done a thousand times before, but it didn't happen."

So, it ended, 10–10.

Still, the consensus after the game was that the conference athletic directors would vote to send Michigan to the Rose Bowl, in large part because the Buckeyes had gone the previous year and were beaten, 42–17, by Southern Cal.

The vote was never made public and the documents have ironically disappeared from conference offices. But it went in favor of Ohio State—with former Wolverine hockey player and then Michigan State AD Burt Smith admitting he voted for the Buckeyes—and the feeling was that Franklin's injury played a big part in their decision.

Franklin was sacked by All-America defensive end Van Ness DeCree with 2:20 remaining and suffered a broken collarbone. "I heard something pop and knew something was wrong right away," Franklin said afterward.

He was disgusted that his team was denied Pasadena, and later said, "For sure, I could've played."

Schembechler told reporters: "I'm very bitter. I resent it. It's the lowest day of my athletic career."

He brought his Wolverines together that Sunday to pay tribute to and console them.

"Bo was in tears," said Lantry. "It was real somber, like somebody had died."

Franklin said, "I never, ever saw Bo that upset."

However, something good came from that debacle. The Big Ten realized how archaic its bowl rule was, and began allowing multiple teams to accept invitations. The first beneficiary was the 1975 Wolverines, who went to the Orange Bowl.

"But it was at a hell of an expense," said Schembechler, who never got over the class of Franklin and Lantry going 30–2–1 and never playing in a bowl.

Lantry said, "When we filmed that documentary *Tiebreaker*, Gradishar was sitting right across from me at the table. I looked at one of the producers and said, 'What in the hell are you doing? Is there some meaning to this?' He said, 'Well, sort of.' That's right where he was coming at me from in that game."

The teams met in 2013 at the Blackwell Hotel, just a short distance from Ohio Stadium in Columbus, to break bread and do an in-meal interview for *Tiebreaker*.

Those Buckeyes and Wolverines had been pitted against one another for decades, but Lantry and Hicks helped organize golf outings and dinners for them all to "bury the hatchet" and share the bond of the rivalry. Lantry said they discovered that because the Buckeyes played for Woody Hayes and the Wolverines for his former assistant, Schembechler, they had much in common.

Hicks, who died in 2016, became good friends with Lantry, who attended his funeral with several other Wolverines. Lantry, smiling, said Hicks always insisted that he didn't pull down the banner back in '73.

Lantry became Michigan's career leader at the time in field goals (21), extra points (113), and kick scoring (176 points). But those kicks he missed and the 33-yard attempt he missed in a 12–10 loss to the Buckeyes in 1974 are what he's generally remembered for.

However, Lantry should be remembered for far more than that.

He fought in Vietnam, returned to walk on the football team at Michigan, and kicked the game-winning field goal against Purdue that sealed a share of the 1972 Big Ten championship for the Wolverines.

Lantry graduated with a degree in education in 1975 and was married while beginning to raise his family as an upperclassman. He kicked briefly in the NFL for the Dallas Cowboys before leaving both the military and athletics behind. He established Lantry and Associates, Inc., in 2000, and provides automated systems for assembly lines to Detroit's automotive industry.

He was vilified by some fans for those missed kicks while being admired by "thousands" of others whose letters of inspiration still fill boxes at his home in Bloomfield Hills, Michigan, and can bring him to tears. Dick Vitale, then the new basketball coach at the University of Detroit, and NBC-TV's Joe Garagiola were among those sending letters of encouragement.

"The people who wrote those letters had shocking empathy for me," Lantry said. "Many of them began with, 'You served your country...' And they were very taken aback. They compared my situation to their life's tragedies—even deaths in their families.

"At that time, it meant everything to me. I wanted to be consoled. Family and friends can only do so much of that. The letters usually ended, 'You'll do well in life. Don't let this setback get you down.' And I appreciated it so much. And while missing that last kick was the last thing I did in intercollegiate athletics, it wasn't a tragedy."

Tragedy was the carnage he witnessed in the Mekong River Delta and along the Cambodian border.

Lantry, a member of the Army's 3rd Brigade, 82nd Airborne Division, was honored as the "Veteran of the Game" during the 2017 Ohio State matchup. He waved from the end zone after being introduced, and the Michigan Stadium faithful gave him a rousing ovation.

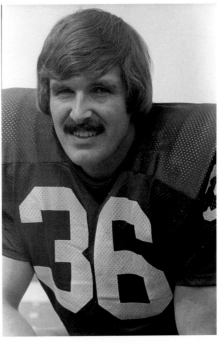

Michigan placekicker Mike Lantry, a Vietnam veteran, set records at Michigan but also missed what could've been the winning field goal in the infamous 10–10 tie with Ohio State in 1973. Lantry went on to become a highly successful businessman and returned to the 2017 game with Ohio State to a standing ovation.
*Courtesy of Bentley Historical Library, University of Michigan.*

That was a different kind of tiebreaker, one that told Lantry that Wolverine fans were in no way ambivalent toward him. They honored his rising above the disappointment of some critical games to succeed in life, while becoming an example of the power of the human spirit.

## Rob Lytle, Tailback Extraordinaire

Michigan coach Jim Harbaugh was a ball boy on the sidelines when he watched Rob Lytle run for the Wolverines, and Lytle's prowess as a fleet runner and punishing blocker brought about a sense of awe from young Harbaugh. He also admired

Lytle for the kind of guy he was, always nice to kids like him and considerate of others.

And when Harbaugh pictures a running back, he can't imagine one much better than Lytle.

"He was just a hard runner," said Harbaugh. "When I think of backs going through the line of scrimmage and lowering their pads, and the way he could run, low off the ground, like an arrow going through snow. That's how I visualize a running back. He was a great running back.

"In that movie, *Everybody's All-American*, he was played by Dennis Quaid. When he [Quaid's character] was playing football, Rob Lytle was the back they used footage of Dennis Quaid being. I always thought that was really neat."

Quaid played Gavin Grey, a fictional All-American running back nicknamed "The Grey Ghost," who concluded his career with the Denver Broncos. NFL footage of Lytle, wearing No. 41 for the Broncos, is used in the 1988 film.

Lytle was a real-life All-American at Michigan in 1976 and was one of Coach Bo Schembechler's absolute favorite players. Harbaugh's father, Jack, coached on Schembechler's staff when Lytle played and dominated games.

His career rushing record of 3,317 yards stood until Butch Woolfolk surpassed it in 1981, and his single-season mark of 1,469 yards lasted twenty-one years before Jamie Morris broke it with 1,703 in 1987.

Lytle, who died of a heart attack in 2010 at the age of fifty-six, was inducted posthumously into the College Football Hall of Fame in 2015.

He was all about family, team, and meeting challenges.

His wife, Tracy, and his son, Kelly, say they couldn't have had a better husband or father. They treasured the family life they had in Fremont, Ohio, where Rob and Tracy met as high school track team sprinters before attending college together in Ann Arbor.

The Wolverines won three Big Ten championships from 1974 to '76, finishing in the Top 10 each season, with Lytle leading the way. He finished third in Heisman Trophy voting as a senior behind Pitt's Tony Dorsett and Southern Cal's Ricky Bell, and he was named the Big Ten's MVP that season.

Lytle definitely met the challenge Michigan's legendary coach put to him straight when he visited campus as a senior at Fremont High.

Kelly said, "Here was Bo Schembechler's recruiting pitch to my dad: 'Rob, we have seven tailbacks here at Michigan. And when you come here, you will be number eight. What happens is up to you.'"

His son, who also played running back at Fremont, chuckled after repeating that line.

"Bo put that kind of challenge in front of my dad," said Kelly, "and he rose to the challenge."

It was a challenge met that took him all the way to the College Football Hall of Fame, where he joined three-time All-American wide receiver Anthony Carter as the only Michigan skill position players since the Schembechler era began to be enshrined there.

"This honor is incredible for dad," said Kelly, who wrote a book, *To Dad, From Kelly*, inspired by letters he wrote to his father after his death to help with his grieving. "And if he could have given his own speech, Dad would say, 'This only happened to me because of the great teams I played on. This is a team accomplishment.'

"Michigan was the perfect match for his personality. He played for a coach who stressed, 'The team, the team, the team.' And my dad was a player who loved his team and teammates."

Kelly spoke on his father's behalf in a ceremony before the Hall of Fame enshrinement, and Tracy represented him on stage during the induction at a New York City hotel ballroom.

"Rob would be very ecstatic about being in the Hall of Fame," said Tracy. "Yet, he was so humble that he never thought of himself as that good. He did it for the

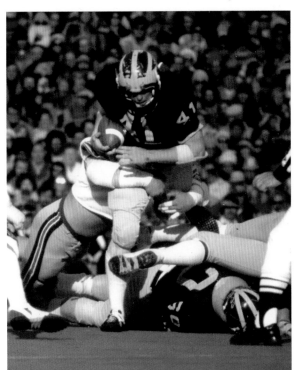

Rob Lytle cuts through the defense in a 1976 game.
*Courtesy of Bentley Historical Library, University of Michigan.*

team and the love of the game. He was a true team player, and even played [nine games] as a fullback."

That wealth of running backs Schembechler mentioned to Lytle as a recruit provided for some truly unique and remarkable backfields. Lytle played in two games in which the Wolverines had a trio of 100-yard rushers:

Part Three

Harlan Huckleby (157), Lytle (105), and Gordon Bell (100) had 362 yards rushing on 40 combined carries (9.1-yard average) against Northwestern in 1975. Huckleby (157), Russell Davis (116), and Lytle (101) totaled 374 on 42 rushes (8.9-yard average) against Stanford in 1976.

Lytle also was highly recruited by Ohio State coach Woody Hayes, and both his wife and son agreed that his favorite win was the 22–0 demolition of the Buckeyes in Columbus in 1976.

"Woody really recruited him hard," said Tracy, a fifth-grade teacher at Lutz Elementary in Fremont. "He'd bring history books over and took the family to dinner. I had a portrait made from a photo of Rob walking off the field the day of that win at Ohio State. His helmet was so banged up and scratched, and there was this light in his eyes. He was really excited and that's how you could tell.

"We went to the Rose Bowl that year after going to the Orange Bowl the previous year. And then Denver went to the Super Bowl in his rookie year! Three straight years of going to bowl games like that was fantastic."

Lytle, a second-round pick by the Broncos in 1977, became the first player to score a touchdown in both the Rose Bowl and Super Bowl. He played seven years in the NFL, and Kelly recalled that his father's right shoulder was hurt so badly after his playing career that he couldn't throw a ball.

"It bothered him that we couldn't play catch, and we'd tease him about that," said Kelly, who graduated from Princeton and ran on its track and field team. "And so he taught himself to throw left-handed so he could be the all-time quarterback in our neighborhood sandlot games. He just loved being a part of our lives.

"He cared. I think that's the best way to summarize Dad. He cared for Mom, my sister [Erin Tober]. He was my best friend. He had a unique charm for being able to make you feel more special. He was fully invested in so many ways."

Lytle was a vice president for the Business Development Office at Old Fort Banking Company in Fremont, and he also found time to be involved in the community.

He was an assistant offensive line coach at Fremont when Charles Woodson, Michigan's 1997 Heisman Trophy winner, played tailback and cornerback.

"Rob was an example and inspiration to all of us who came from small towns that with hard work we, too, could be recognized," Woodson said at the time of Lytle's death. "He never hesitated to share his time with us and help us prepare as we got ready to play the game he loved."

Rick Leach, the Michigan quarterback for Lytle's last two seasons, said, "He was a great competitor and such a great leader. He cared about the team, he cared about Big Ten titles, and would do anything to make the team better."

Lytle did something remarkable, moving to fullback for most of one season to allow Bell and others playing time at tailback. He was totally selfless and never hesitated in doing what was best for the Wolverines.

"My idols were Donnie Dufek and Rob Lytle," said Leach, also noting the Michigan captain his freshman year who was an outstanding safety. "Rob Lytle took me under his wings, and he's no longer here. I loved him like a brother. I think of Robbie awful strong when football season's going on.

"The front of his helmet looked like something that came out of a garbage dump. I mean, I played this one game that Rob went over 100 yards rushing. And when we sat down to watch the film, I had to sit down next to Bo, and he said, 'I want you to watch Rob Lytle. That man had fourteen knock-down blocks, Rick, along with running like he did, and he saved your neck a few times. So you better pay close attention to this man.' When Bo was watching this film, he said, 'This might be one of the greatest college football games I've ever seen a man play.' I think it was Minnesota in my sophomore year. Bo said, 'That's what a Michigan man does, right there.'"

At the end of that season, Lytle, then a senior, beat Ohio State in 1976 for the only time in his career after one tie and two losses. It was a blowout for the Wolverines in Columbus in one of the most offensively imbalanced thrashings you will ever see. Michigan had 366 yards on the ground and zero in the air.

"So he loved number seven," said Leach, who wore that number, "and Rob Lytle was like a man possessed in that game. He ran for 165 yards.

"I threw only six passes and four of them were throwaways before the half. I threw two, maybe three, legitimate passes in that game."

Lytle, Davis, Huckleby, and Leach spearheaded a running game that averaged 5.2 yards per carry that afternoon.

When they returned to Ann Arbor, someone had left champagne on ice at their apartment. It was a game to celebrate in a career to celebrate forever.

## Rick Leach, "The Guts and Glue of the Maize and Blue"

Bob Ufer, excitable and passionate, announced games with exclamation points.

Ufer would lean into his radio microphone at Michigan football games after quarterback Rick Leach inspired him with his play, and proclaim: "Rick Leach— The Guts and Glue of the Maize and Blue!"

If Leach scored a touchdown, Ufer would honk his General George Patton Jeep horn three times, and it was a moment of pure euphoria. That horn, as Ufer

Legendary Michigan radio voice Bob Ufer, who nicknamed Rick Leach "The Guts and Glue of the Maize and Blue," is shown holding the Gen. George Patton horn he honked during games in this 1975 photo.
*Courtesy of Bentley Historical Library, University of Michigan.*

once explained on a broadcast, was a gift to him from Patton's nephew, a devoted listener from Benton Harbor, Michigan, who was given the horn in his uncle's will. You can't make this stuff up.

Ufer, a world-record-setting quarter-miler at Michigan in his youth, loved his Wolverines and really loved Leach and spoke of him as if he was Superman under center.

What did the "Guts and Glue" tag mean to Leach?

"I treasure the relationship I had with Bob Ufer as a player and in the years after that," said Leach. "Bob knew the history, tradition, and all the background stories. There were a few guys through the years that put a little gleam in his eye, and he gave some players nicknames.

"I'll be forever thankful for the nickname he gave me—that's for sure!"

Leach related that Ufer, an Ann Arbor insurance salesman during the week and a wild entertainer on football Saturdays, actually was part of Coach Bo Schembechler's recruitment of Leach.

"Bob had a unique way," said Leach. "He got me on the side and said, 'Look, your dad came to Michigan, Bo wants you here at Michigan, and you look at your background, and you just get your name on that paper and come to Michigan! Hah!'"

Ufer pointed out that Leach's father, Dick, was the catcher for the Wolverines' NCAA championship baseball team in 1953, and that Richard Max Leach was born in University of Michigan Hospital. Leach, he stated matter-of-factly, was born to quarterback this team.

Rick wanted to play for Michigan, no doubt about it. But there was one snag in signing that national letter of intent to play football. Leach said Schembechler didn't want two-sport athletes, particularly at quarterback, a position that required more time and practice than any other position.

"If Bo hadn't relented," said Leach, "I probably was going to go to the University of Arizona to play football for Jim Young, who had been on Bo's staff at Michigan, and play for a great baseball program there, too.

"I loved baseball and many thought that was my best sport to play down the road professionally. I had to play both sports."

Leach, All-State in baseball, basketball, and football at Flint Southwestern, did something quite amazing as a true freshman. He ran Schembechler's vaunted option attack despite never having run that offense in high school, mastering it quicker than seemed possible.

He explained that it was made possible by making the two-hour roundtrip drive from Flint to Ann Arbor three days every week in the summer of 1975 to work with the Michigan coaches and study film. Leach acquired the technique and knowledge necessary to hit the ground running and had the great athletic ability and toughness to make it work.

Schembechler marveled at how Leach only had to be taught something one time to retain it. That was key to his early success.

Leach set the NCAA record with 82 touchdowns accounted for, set the Big Ten records for total offense (6,460 yards) and touchdown passes (48), and finished third in Heisman Trophy voting while being named the Big Ten MVP as a senior in 1978.

"He is the best football player in the United States of America," Schembechler proclaimed.

Leach won three Big Ten titles, beat Ohio State three times after losing as a freshman, and was named the co-MVP of the 1979 Rose Bowl even though the Wolverines lost to USC.

What of all that meant the most to him?

"There is only one stat that means more than anything to me," said Leach. "I was there for forty-eight games and started forty-seven of the forty-eight and played the majority of the other game.

"So I answered the bell every week. How many guys will do that today?"

He got his bell rung as a freshman in the 1976 Orange Bowl against a great Oklahoma team but returned to action.

Leach did not practice the week before the reunion game with Notre Dame in 1978, when an ankle injury kept him from participating in everything except the Friday walk-through practice.

"I was held back a half hour after everyone else left after practices that week and had to exit a back door so nobody saw that I was hurt," Leach said. "Bob Ufer was around, and I told him I wouldn't be able to play. And Bob cried! But I was just pulling his chain, and I told him I would find a way to play."

The matchup was being hyped to the max. It was the first game between the winningest teams in college football after a thirty-five-year separation and featured Heisman Trophy candidates in Leach and Joe Montana.

Leach struggled early but pulled out the game with three second-half touchdown passes—two to tight end Doug Marsh and one to wingback Ralph Clayton—in a 28–14 win by the Wolverines.

Montana ended up completing 16 of 29 passes for 192 yards, while Leach had eight completions in 20 attempts for 110 yards. But it was Leach who made the passes count, as Montana ended up factoring into only one touchdown.

Montana and Leach got to know one another better during the week leading up to San Francisco's first Super Bowl appearance and win at the Pontiac Silverdome in 1982. Forty-Niners offensive guard Walt Downing played with Leach at Michigan and was looking for a place to get away from the madness of the week.

"So I had some of them over to my house in Farmington Hills," Leach said. "We had a great time. I told Joe, 'Just so your teammates know, I kicked your ass at Notre Dame!' Joe laughed and said, 'Well, one thing is for sure. If you were such a good football player, you would not be playing pro baseball right now.'"

Still, Leach will always have football bragging rights over one of the greatest quarterbacks in NFL history.

Leach was tough and talented, always finding a way to take the field and perform at a high level.

"He is the greatest football player I have ever been associated with," said Schembechler.

That was a powerful compliment.

"You've been around long enough to know the respect and admiration the guys who played for Bo had for him," Leach said. "So for him to make that comment, it still touches my heart."

Leach paused and emotions flowed at the memory of Schembechler, and what the player and coach meant to one another.

"I am just grateful and thankful that I had that four-year window and opportunity to play for that man," said Leach, "and we had great success as a team."

Michigan finished in the Associated Press Top 10 final rankings every season he played, and Leach's play stayed with people. When *Sports Illustrated* ranked "The 50 Greatest Sports Figures From Michigan" at the end of the last century, Leach was No. 22 on a list that included Detroit pro athletes and all college figures.

It took time for him to get on a roll, though.

Leach averaged less than nine pass attempts per game in each of his first two seasons, and he had just 16 touchdown passes in that time.

However, Schembechler opened it up somewhat in the next two seasons. Leach averaged 14.5 and then 12.1 pass attempts while throwing 32 touchdown passes. He averaged a TD every tenth time he threw the ball as a junior and senior, and that compares quite favorably with the one touchdown pass in every 15.5 attempts by the current school record holder in career touchdown passes, Chad Henne, as a junior and senior in 2006 and 2007.

Leach said there's a simple answer for the early lack of passing. He said Schembechler believed in the Woody Hayes edict: "Three things can happen when you pass and two of them are bad."

"But Bo got more confidence in calling passes after seeing what we could do," said Leach, whose top receivers—All-America wide receiver Jim Smith, Clayton, and Marsh—each went in either the second or third round of the NFL draft.

Leach was a fifth-round pick by the Denver Broncos but went with baseball because the Detroit Tigers made him their first-round pick in 1979. He went on to play 10 seasons in the majors as an outfielder and first baseman.

The Philadelphia Phillies drafted him both out of high school and after his junior season at Michigan, but he resisted a huge bonus to stay at Michigan and was All-American in both sports as a senior.

"I'll never forget something that happened during my senior year," said Leach. "I'd already signed my letter of intent to come to Michigan, and a lot of baseball scouts were coming around, and a lot of people were talking to my dad. A lot of teams were in agreement to take me in the first round but only if I agreed to go into baseball and forget about football.

"One of the head scouts for the Philadelphia Phillies sat down with us, and he put a number on a piece of paper that definitely caught my attention."

It was $100,000, the total that club was willing to pay Leach in a signing bonus.

"My dad has that scout leave the room at the hotel," Leach recalled. "My dad looked me right in the eye and said, 'I'm going to tell you something. I want you to trust me and what I'm going to tell you. This money, which is a lot of money, when all is said and done, isn't going to mean anything compared to what four years at the University of Michigan will mean. If you do there what you think you can do and play the way you think you can play, this money's not going to mean anything. And if you're good enough and healthy, there will be more money than this waiting for you at the end.'

"And I never forgot that."

Four years later, the Tigers made him their first-round draft pick. He was the 13th overall player selected.

"I signed with the Tigers for $125,000," said Leach. "So what I did in four years of football and baseball at Michigan got me twenty-five grand more than I would've signed for out of high school. And what I got at Michigan, you could never put a price on that."

The personal relationships and friendships he developed in Ann Arbor were beyond priceless.

Leach said his parents called him and "were kind of teary-eyed" when telling him about the letter they received after his senior year from Jim Harbaugh's parents, Jack and Jackie. Rick had befriended the future All-American quarterback and head coach of the Wolverines when he was a young boy running around practices and games. His father coached defensive backs for Schembechler back then.

Leach recalled: "They said, 'Rick, you wouldn't believe this letter. It's thanking you and saying how much all the time spent with Jimmy meant to them as parents.' My parents wrote them a letter back, and all of this was just a treasure.

"For me, it's spiritual in a lot of ways. His dad was coaching when I played. I had a close relationship with Jack even though he was a defensive coach. I call Jack the 'Godfather' of our football program. And then when Jimmy played here, I saw the things in Jimmy that people saw in me. My dad was a coach, and I used to play catch and try to be around the players. Jimmy was the exact same way."

Harbaugh had Leach back as an honorary captain for a game in 2016, and the coach later sent him a moving autographed photo taken by David Turnley of his hero standing and waving there at midfield for the coin toss with Jake Butt, the two-time All-American tight end and co-captain, and fellow captains Chris Wormley and Kenny Allen, representing special teams that day.

The photo is signed:

"Rick,

You've always been a fierce competitor and great leader. It was an honor having a Michigan Man lead us into battle."

The coach signed his full name below it in flowing cursive, each letter completely legible.

Coach Jim Harbaugh had Rick Leach back as an honorary captain for a game in 2016, and the coach later sent him a moving autographed photo taken by football team photographer David Turnley of his hero standing and waving there at midfield for the coin toss with Jake Butt, the two-time All-American tight end and co-captain, and fellow captains Chris Wormley and Kenny Allen, representing special teams that day.
*Photo Courtesy of Rick Leach.*

That's a special story right there.

So was the fact that his running back classmates, Russell Davis and Harlan Huckleby, took the field with him.

"I called and told them both about the honor Coach Harbaugh was blessing me with," Leach recalled, "and I said, 'Gentlemen, we came in together and I'd appreciate it if you could walk out with me. We're going out together.' And we did that and had a wonderful time."

But it's an even more touching story than everyone thought.

"That was the last game my dad ever saw," said Leach, who was overcome with emotion at that memory. "He was so sick, and we weren't even sure if we could get him down there. But they let him sit up in a suite with the family, and it was the last game my dad ever saw."

He recalled how it all began with his father teaching him how to play the games and love Michigan, and he noted that his own three sons graduated from the family alma mater.

"Because of my dad's background," said Leach, "the flavor of Michigan was always prominent around the Leach household."

It's been a long, special relationship between Leach and the Wolverines. He gets emotional talking about his father, Bo, and former teammates. He loves them all so strongly.

"The Guts and Glue of the Maize and Blue."

That's Richard Max Leach, whose aim always has been true.

## Wangler to Carter: The Indiana Miracle

If you said that John Wangler's last-second, near-miracle 45-yard touchdown pass to Anthony Carter on October 27, 1979, was the most dramatic play in the history of Michigan football, you might get a short-lived argument.

The fourth-down touchdown pass from Elvis Grbac to Desmond Howard to clinch the 1991 Notre Dame game was great. So was Scott Dreisbach's game-winning pass to Mercury Hayes on the final play of a 1995 game with Virginia. Charles Woodson's and Desmond Howard's punt return touchdowns against Ohio State in their Heisman Trophy-winning seasons would get mentioned, too.

But it's hard to pick against Wangler-to-Carter because it probably incited more joy and lasting memories than any other Michigan play.

Radio play-by-play man Bob Ufer gets an assist in that regard because his horn-honking, crying, shouting, and hyperbole on the call of the play and its aftermath were so spontaneous and endearing. It lives on in YouTube replays that will forever freeze in time the high drama that played out on that cool, cloudy autumn afternoon at Michigan Stadium.

The Wolverines and Hoosiers were knotted at 21-all with six seconds remaining to play and the ball on the Indiana 45 yard line. Coach Bo Schembechler put his left arm around Wangler on the sideline and barked out the play—"54 Pass Post!"—before Wangler jogged into the huddle to call the play.

Wangler said: "As Anthony was breaking the huddle, he said, 'Throw me the ball. I'm going to be open.' I said, 'I am. Don't worry about it.'"

Each of Wangler's top three options on the play, though, was a future NFL starter.

"Ralph Clayton was running down the one sideline straight to the end zone," said Wangler, "and Doug Marsh was on the other side as the tight end, and then Alan Mitchell was out there, too. Anthony was the one who was going to do the post route."

Wangler made the obligatory play fake to his star tailback before dropping back to pass.

"The ironic thing is that I had to reverse-pivot and fake an off-tackle play to Butch Woolfolk, right?" Wangler recalled with a chuckle. "They are in a prevent defense, and you aren't fooling anyone with a fake. I always teased Bo about that. But the next year we put in the drop-back and even some shotguns for that kind of Hail Mary situation."

Wangler wasn't pressured in the pocket and fired a tight spiral down the middle of the field that Carter caught in front of two defensive backs at the 20 yard line. Neither was able to corral him, and another Indiana defensive back made an attempt to get Carter with a diving tackle but ended up prone on the ground, face down and arms extended, having come up empty at the 3 yard line.

Wangler said: "There weren't too many human beings walking around on the earth that could've caught the ball and maintained his balance and avoided three tacklers who had great angles on him. Tim Wilbur, who was an All-Big Ten (defensive back), had a really good angle on him and didn't get him. His knee was really close to the ground, and it really opened everybody's eyes to what a special talent he was, getting into the end zone after all of that."

Carter caught 17 passes as a freshman and seven went for touchdowns. He averaged a phenomenal 27.2 yards per catch in his first season and was an All-American in each of the next three seasons.

He established a Big Ten record with 37 touchdown catches, but none was more famous than this one.

Part Three

Carter appeared to mimic the touchdown call of the official in the end zone, extending both arms high with the ball in his right hand and prancing with his knees repeatedly bouncing up high like a marching band drum major.

Schembechler actually bounded for joy in a rare show of glee.

"Obviously," said Wangler, "to win the game was important. But to see the emotion Bo had jumping up and down on the sidelines and going crazy was something special."

Wangler said he can't remember Schembechler having that level of joy on the field after any other game in his coaching career.

"And then everybody was mobbing Anthony in the end zone," said Wangler. "I was actually running down the field to try to call a time-out because I didn't think he was going to get in, and maybe we'd have enough time to kick a field goal. But once I saw him get through a couple guys, I thought he might be able to pull this off. He got into the end zone, and the pile got so big that people were hyperventilating and getting pulled out. So I just ran right to the tunnel to get out of there."

Carter said Woolfolk was "trying to throw everyone off of me" in the end zone and noted that he couldn't breathe until his tailback took action.

"You can't draw that up," said Wangler. "I tell people, 'The way Bob Ufer called it was probably better than the play.' He immortalized it with his call and nobody could do it like Ufe."

Ufer described the play, honking his Jeep horn repeatedly and at times becoming inaudible in his excitement, before connecting Michigan's greatest coaches in the moment:

> "Anthony Carter, the human torpedo, caught the pass. Bo Schembechler is looking up at Fielding H. Yost in football's Valhalla, and Bo Schembechler says, 'Thank you, Fielding Yost! Thank you, Fielding Yost for that one!' Look at the crowd. You cannot believe it! Michigan throws a 45-yard touchdown pass. Johnny Wangler to Anthony Carter will be heard until another 100 years of Michigan football is played."

Carter, in a radio interview years later, said listening to the call still gives him "goose bumps and chills" and he noted that it was the greatest play of his high school, college, or pro career.

"It still seems like yesterday," Carter told AnnArbor.com on the thirtieth anniversary of the play in 2009. "People still talk about it, and so that's a great indication of what that play really meant.

Photographer Robert Kalmbach captured the sequences of Anthony Carter's (No. 1) dramatic 45-yard touchdown catch on the final play of Michigan's 27–21 win over Indiana in 1979.
1: Carter catches the pass from quarterback John Wangler on a slant route in the middle of the field.
2: Carter regains his balance after a near fall and sprints toward the end zone.
3: Carter extends his right hand while crossing the goal line with the ball cradled in his left hand.
4: Tailback Butch Woolfolk embraces Carter, who is holding the ball aloft, in the end zone prior to a dog pile celebration.
*Photos by Robert Kalmbach.*
*Courtesy of Bentley Historical Library, University of Michigan.*

"It's one of those plays that people are always going to remember. No matter what happens with Michigan football, people are always going to remember that one particular play."

Wangler said, "Just to be part of that memorable play was obviously one of the highlights of my athletic career. The way it unfolded—we weren't really used to throwing the ball much in those days and were just evolving into a passing team."

Wangler, then a junior, didn't even start the Indiana game. He alternated that year with B.J. Dickey, who ran effectively against the Hoosiers but struggled in throwing the ball and had one interception. Wangler came on to complete 10 of 14 throws for 163 yards and the historic touchdown pass.

He clicked with Carter that year, and they appeared headed for a record-setting game against North Carolina in the Gator Bowl. Wangler had completed 6 of 8 passes for 203 yards with a 53-yard touchdown to Carter. However, midway through the second quarter, North Carolina linebacker terror Lawrence Taylor sacked Wangler, who could be heard writhing in pain. Wangler had torn knee ligaments, and his career was in doubt.

Wangler worked tirelessly on his rehab in the weight room. He made it back to the starting lineup the following season with what was called a "courageous and remarkable comeback" by Schembechler.

(Left to Right) Quarterback John Wangler, receiver Anthony Carter, and Coach Bo Schembechler discuss a play on the sideline in a 1979 game. *Courtesy of Bentley Historical Library, University of Michigan.*

His college career had a storybook ending. Wangler completed 12 of 20 passes for 145 yards and a 7-yard touchdown to Carter for a 23–6 win over Washington in the Rose Bowl on January 1, 1981. It was the first bowl victory for Schembechler.

"John Wangler, who I've had a great friendship and relationship with, I think of as I think of no other quarterback," said Rick Leach, his predecessor as the Michigan quarterback. "And I always tell Johnny, 'Gosh darn you, Johnny, you were the first quarterback to bring Bo his Rose Bowl victory, and I fought my rear end off and could never get it done.' And John Wangler did, and I love him to death for it."

That 1980 team finished 10–2, with early-season losses at Notre Dame by two points and to South Carolina and Heisman Trophy–winning tailback George Rogers by three points. That win in Pasadena was the Wolverines' ninth straight. They closed out the Big Ten season with three consecutive shutouts and a 9–3 win at Ohio State before dominating the talented Huskies.

Schembechler often said he believed that was his finest team.

"Bo said that about us and you hate to make comparisons," said Wangler. "But by the end of that year, with what we could do with a great offensive line, Anthony and some great running backs, and we had a defense that didn't give up touchdowns.

"We were playing as well as anybody in the country. We stumbled early, but got on a nice roll and turned it around. If there was a playoff, I think we would've been hard to beat. It was a special season, and we had great chemistry. Everybody got along and played better than some people thought we could, and we were able to finish on a real high note."

The passing combo that made its name in the '79 Indiana game helped Schembechler get his long-awaited ride off the field on the shoulders of his players in Pasadena in their final game together.

## Anthony Carter, No. 1 in Every Way

Anthony Carter caught the football and seemed to dare defenders: "Catch me if you can."

A.C. was a blur who seemed to have one step on everyone even before the footrace began. He was a wisp, only 5-foot-11 and 160 pounds, and there wasn't that much of him to grab, either.

But there is a whole lot of him in the record books and was a whole lot of him in end zones during a fabulous career. Carter became only the second three-time All-American in school history from 1980 to 1982, joining end Bennie Oosterbaan, who preceded him by fifty-five years.

Bo Schembechler beamed with a special pride whenever A.C. was mentioned. Schembechler called him "the finest receiver in the nation" and noted, "Nobody can allow Carter to have single coverage."

Carter realized he was a game-breaker beginning with the first games he played as a ten-year-old in Riviera Beach, Florida.

"Every time I got the football, I ended up in the end zone," Carter told the *Washington Post* during his college career. "So I thought this must be my game."

Carter reached the end zone more often than any receiver in Big Ten history, catching 37 touchdown passes, a mark that stood twenty-two years until Michigan's Braylon Edwards surpassed it by two.

Part Three

Anthony Carter grabs a pass in 1981, his second of three consecutive All-American seasons.
*Courtesy of Bentley Historical Library, University of Michigan.*

A.C.'s school marks of 161 catches for 3,076 yards also stood until Braylon, the son of his college teammate, tailback Stanley Edwards, came along.

And his single-season record of 14 touchdown catches in 1980 remained until 1991 Heisman Trophy winner Desmond Howard broke it with 19. Carter, by the way, finished in the Top 10 in Heisman voting three times, coming in fourth in 1982.

It's noteworthy that the Big Ten Network, in 2014, placed him on the Michigan football Mount Rushmore along with the school's three Heisman winners, Tom Harmon (1940), Howard, and Charles Woodson (1997).

A.C. could do it all.

He also was a superb kick returner, taking back 63 kickoffs for 1,606 yards (26.3-yard average) and 79 punts for 907 yards (11.5-yard average) and two touchdowns. His school-record 5,799 yards in all-purpose yardage stood until tailback/returner Jamie Morris broke it in 1987.

That was a little over three miles as a receiver and returner for Carter, who rushed 36 times for 213 yards and another touchdown.

No. 1 was No. 1 in so many statistical categories that were eventually eclipsed. However, he will always be the receiver who made No. 1 the number every receiver at Michigan, including Edwards, coveted wearing. Schembechler once sweetened the pot for Greg McMurtry, a Boston Red Sox first-round pick out of Brockton (Massachusetts) High, by offering him No. 1 if he became a Wolverine, which he did.

The legend of Anthony Carter began on October 27, 1979, against Indiana.

Quarterback John Wangler's 45-yard touchdown pass to Carter on the final play that afternoon is arguably the most memorable moment in Michigan football history. With the score tied and six seconds remaining, A.C. caught Wangler's spiral in front of two defensive backs at the 20 yard line, made them miss, and eluded an ankle tackle at the 3 yard line to reach the end zone, knees bounding high as he held the ball aloft. Michigan Stadium turned into a Mardi Gras scene.

"Anthony was just a young freshman," said Wangler, "and that play really put him on the map as far as being one of the greatest ever to play the position in college football. That really opened everyone's eyes."

There were plenty of big games ahead. Carter finished with a Wolverines record 14 100-yard games, and his highest total was 156 against Illinois in 1981. A.C. had four catches for 141 yards and two touchdowns in the 1979 Gator Bowl. He made six catches for 127 yards and a touchdown against UCLA in the 1981 Bluebonnet Bowl win.

Many of the next generation of Wolverines receivers, including Braylon Edwards, grew up wanting to emulate A.C.

John Kolesar, who caught the game-winning passes against Ohio State in 1988 and in the 1988 Hall of Fame Bowl, was one of those who grew up idolizing Carter.

"When I was in ninth grade, we used to play Sunday pickup games at the high school," said Kolesar. "I used to have two plays—A.C. right and A.C. left."

Carter could do more than run and deke, though. He also had tremendous hands and hand-eye coordination.

There was a catch against Purdue that doesn't get much recall, but it was exceptional in regard to that focus and sure-handedness.

The Boilermakers defensive back tipped the long pass, but Carter's eyes stayed on the ball as it fluttered. He caught it over his shoulder and initially bobbled it before securing it and sprinting to the end zone.

Nobody seemed to be able to stop him, and there were even a few days when Schembechler had to play catch-up with Carter, who got homesick in freshman camp and returned home to Riviera Beach.

Schembechler reached him on the phone and believed their conversation would bring the desired result.

"I didn't think he was gone for good," Schembechler told *Sports Illustrated*'s Doug Looney in 1981. "He just needed to go home for a little reinforcement from his family and friends. And the reinforcement he got was, 'Get your ass back up there right now.'"

Carter's mother, among others, told him to honor his commitment and return to the Wolverines rather than transfer closer to home at Florida State. He listened, and the hard to cover receiver blossomed into the 1982 Big Ten MVP and a team tri-captain in that senior season.

His elusiveness continued serving him well as one of pro football's top pass-catchers. A.C. led the Michigan Panthers to the 1983 USFL championship and had 160 catches for 3,042 yards and 27 touchdowns playing three seasons in that upstart league. He then spent 11 seasons in the NFL with 7,733 yards and 55 touchdowns via the air.

The touchdowns that came so naturally to him as a young boy playing on the dusty sandlots never ceased coming his way.

Carter caught 119 touchdown passes over his entire college and pro career.

But that one TD scamper against the Hoosiers in '79—which Wangler noted "put him on the map"—remains the crème de la crème from the A.C. files.

Jim Brandstatter, the long-time radio voice of Michigan football said, "Anthony Carter was the most humble of kids. You never thought he could do what he did, but Anthony was just magical."

## Jim Harbaugh Begins a Quarterback Tradition

There are game changers, and then there are program changers.

Jim Harbaugh was both. He transformed the Michigan program from its three-yards-and-a-cloud-of-dust era and moved it toward the pro-style offense that was installed four years after his All-America senior season of 1986.

The Wolverines did far more than win with Harbaugh, who was 21–3–1 and beat Ohio State in his final two seasons. They turned the page in terms of offensive style as he became Coach Bo Schembechler's one and only quarterback to be a first-round NFL draft pick, opening the door for eight future NFL passers at Michigan in the two decades that followed.

James Joseph Harbaugh turned Michigan into a passing school, and amazingly did so while running Schembechler's option attack that required precision pitches and keepers by the quarterback. However, Schembechler knew what he had in Harbaugh and also incorporated post routes and out-cut passes to take advantage of his quarterback's strong, accurate arm.

Assistant coach Cam Cameron, the future head coach at Indiana and of the Miami Dolphins, would mentor Harbaugh and then went all-out to implement the pro-style passing approach with Gary Moeller in 1990, when he replaced Schembechler. Jerry Hanlon, best known as an ultra-successful offensive line coach, coached quarterbacks for several years and also had a great impact on Harbaugh.

Harbaugh's 387 pass completions, 62.4 percent completion rate, and 5,449 passing yards all topped the school's career passing lists when he graduated. And he basically set those marks in two seasons by throwing for 2,729 yards as a senior and 1,976 as a junior. Steve Smith's 1,735 yards in 1982 had been the single-season record.

Elvis Grbac, Todd Collins, Scott Dreisbach, and Brian Griese followed Harbaugh to the NFL as accomplished passers in the 1990s. Then Tom Brady came off a strong senior season at Michigan to establish himself as perhaps the game's greatest all-time quarterback in the first two decades of a new century. Chad Henne also became a solid pro quarterback, and John Navarre and Drew Henson made it to the NFL. So did 2010 All-America Denard Robinson, who moved to running back in the pros after running the spread offense for Coach Rich Rodriquez during a brief lapse from a true passing approach in Ann Arbor.

Grbac broke all of Harbaugh's career records and also set the school touchdown passing mark with 71, a full 40 more than Harbaugh, who ranked seventh in school career passing yardage upon returning to coach his alma mater in 2015.

The whole Michigan experience has truly been a case of living the dream for Harbaugh, who grew up about one mile from the Big House on Anderson Avenue while attending elementary, middle, and high schools in Ann Arbor in the 1970s. His father, Jack, was an assistant coach for the Wolverines before he moved on to Stanford as defensive coordinator during Jim's sophomore year at Ann Arbor Pioneer High.

Jim and his older brother, John, who beat him and the San Francisco 49ers in the Super Bowl as head coach of the Baltimore Ravens, rode their bikes to Wolverines practices after school and lived for the games. Placekicker Mike Lantry recalled the Harbaugh boys having the game-day chore of keeping Schembechler's electrical lines for communication purposes untangled as he made abrupt moves during sideline rants.

The boys loved it when their heroes, such as quarterback Rick Leach or cornerback Dave Brown, played catch with them or threw them a wristband.

When Leach was asked about those days with "Jimmy," as he and others back then still refer to Harbaugh, he chuckled and said, "You mean the little guy that John Wangler and I used to tape up in the locker to give him more air? Bo would come over and ask, 'Where is Jimmy?' I'd say, 'I have no idea.'"

Was "Jimmy" that much of a distraction?

"Well," said Leach, "Let's put it this way. He wanted to ask you questions about why you were doing this, why you were doing that. He'd want to play catch all the time. And if you were having a rough day with Bo, you didn't want little Jimmy in your back pocket that day, right?"

Part Three

It was their mother, Jackie Harbaugh, who convinced Millie Schembechler (Bo's wife) that the children of coaches should be allowed to attend practices in order to be around their fathers, who worked long hours.

"That's Jim Harbaugh when he was one of our ball boys! I must have kicked him out of a hundred practices."

Ball boy Jim Harbaugh congratulates his hero, Michigan 1978 All-America quarterback Rick Leach, after a touchdown. *Courtesy of Bentley Historical Library, University of Michigan.*

The time with the team allowed them to dream big dreams while having the kind of experiences few youngsters realize.

Schembechler returned to his office after practice one day to find young Jimmy leaning back in his office chair with his feet atop the desk.

"How are *you*, Jim Harbaugh?" Bo bellowed, thinking this would scare the living daylights out of him.

Only the kid didn't flinch, move, or react with anything beyond his friendly reply:

"Fine. How are you, Bo?"

Bo loved retelling that story once Harbaugh became his quarterback.

"I knew I had a future quarterback, a future leader, right then and there. That kid had moxie!"

He did need to be harnessed, though.

"Harbaugh was an ornery little devil," Bo continued. "He was a stubborn but playful kid who was always in the locker room or on the sidelines. He had a temper that he had to learn to control, though. We couldn't have a coach *and* a quarterback with a bad temper.

"But I knew the Harbaugh kid had a special flair for competing. Most of the coaches who recruited him out of Palo Alto [California] knew him as a kid. They knew he could be a leader, and that's why they went after Jim."

Harbaugh visited schools where he knew the coaches through his father—Stanford, Arizona, and Wisconsin in addition to Michigan. Cal-Berkeley was his only visit to a school lacking personal ties. In fact, Dave McClain, then the Badgers' coach, was once his babysitter.

"I knew that Dave McClain thought a California quarterback would make his program," Harbaugh said while playing at Michigan. "People think quarterbacks from California have an extra finger or something. But the seven-on-seven passing leagues they have there do make a difference. You play twenty games of touch football with nothing but throwing. They keep stats, and it's big like American Legion baseball is here."

Harbaugh spent the last two years of high school at Palo Alto High and played American Legion baseball, too. One of his teammates was a catcher named Bob Melvin, who went on to play and manage in the major leagues. Jim also hung out at Stanford practices.

Harbaugh, who would become the head coach at Stanford before going to the Niners, added, "And I got to throw with John Elway, Steve Dils, and Turk Schonert to guys like Ken Margerum."

They all played for Stanford either before or while his father coached there, and Jim tried to emulate Elway, who shared quarterback tips with him.

He also learned life lessons in California.

"I always loved sports," Harbaugh said. "But I had no self-control until I got to Palo Alto. I got along better with the people out there because they are so easygoing. But I guess I grew up, too. I figured I couldn't act like a jerk because I wouldn't have any friends.

"I went to a high school there that was full of kids with a lot of money. Most of their parents were tied to Stanford in some way. They influenced me to do better in school. And I knew I couldn't go to a good school because my grades wouldn't be good enough."

In addition to all his playing honors at Michigan, Harbaugh also was named to the Big Ten All-Academic team.

He chose the school he'd dreamed about since he was a young boy to play for Schembechler. Jim loved every minute of it, too. He got around town in a beat-up, red Volkswagen beetle that he customized when the gear shift knob broke by drilling a hole into a baseball and fitting it onto the shifter. He ate Blimpy Burgers and roomed with linebacker and fellow 1986 co-captain Andy Moeller, his Pioneer teammate and longtime friend whose father, Gary, also was an assistant coach at Michigan when his father was.

Still, the player-coach relationship between Harbaugh and Schembechler got off to a rocky start. Jim didn't know what to make of Bo, who got on him hard as he did all players while molding him. Jim actually thought Bo "hated" him before realizing that he only challenged the players he saw as having the potential to make an impact.

He redshirted in 1982, played sparingly behind Smith in 1983, and didn't get to start until 1984, when he broke his arm early in the season against Michigan State.

"Back when I was a true freshman or a sophomore or even a redshirt sophomore," Harbaugh said, "I wasn't a finished product by any means. Don't think I could've even have gone out there as a true freshman."

Smith was a quality quarterback, and he allowed Harbaugh to develop over two seasons. Schembechler needed Harbaugh to step up when the time came perhaps as much as any quarterback he ever coached.

Had Harbaugh not developed into a difference-maker, there was little reason to believe either of his backups, Chris Zurbrugg or Russ Rein, would have led the Wolverines to greatness. Their talent levels were nowhere near Harbaugh's, and Michigan went 3–5 beginning with the game in which he was injured and out for the rest of the 1984 season. The Wolverines were 3–1 in games Harbaugh started, even beating the top-ranked Miami Hurricanes, and finished 6–6 overall.

He led Michigan to a final No. 2 ranking in 1985 and a Big Ten championship in 1986. The Wolverines were so close to the ultimate season in Harbaugh's senior year. They were undefeated and on the verge of perfection and a possible national championship.

However, in Harbaugh's final game at Michigan Stadium, Michigan fell victim to an upset by Minnesota, 20–17.

So when Harbaugh spoke to reporters two days later and five days before playing the Buckeyes, he dropped the prediction to end all predictions: "I guarantee we will beat Ohio State and be in Pasadena New Year's Day. People

Jim Harbaugh throws a touchdown pass to tailback Gerald White against Oregon State in 1986.
*Photo by Robert Kalmbach.*
*Courtesy of Bentley Historical Library, University of Michigan.*

might not give us a snowball's chance in hell to beat them in Columbus, but we're going to. We don't care where we play the game. I hate to say it, but we could play at noon or midnight. We're going to be jacked up, and we're going to win."

Schembechler's reaction to the bold prediction was another surprise. He hated gift-wrapped bulletin board material—especially on the week of "The Game"—but presented a united front.

When asked about the boast that same Monday at his Weber's Inn press luncheon, Schembechler said he wouldn't want a quarterback who would think otherwise and completely diffused the coach-quarterback controversy everyone anticipated. Bo was old-school and stressed letting your play speak for itself. But instead of squashing Harbaugh's bravado, he lauded it.

"I didn't know what Bo would say about it," Harbaugh said. "But from the time I was a little kid, I wanted to play in the Rose Bowl. I saw it as my destiny. I went to three Rose Bowls and walked the sideline as a kid. Michigan needed to win that game to get there, and it was my last chance—the last chance for a lot of us. We had to win, and that's how I felt about it.

"Bo pulled me into the area where the coaches dress for practice that Monday, and he reacted a lot better than I expected. He looked at me and said, 'Well, you shot your mouth off again.' I said, 'Yes, I did.' And then he just said, 'Well, we're going to have to back it up for you.' And then, in front of the team, Bo said, 'I know one guy who thinks we can win this game and it's our quarterback!'

"He had my back, and that felt so good."

Michigan won, 26–24, after Buckeyes placekicker Matt Frantz hooked a 45-yard field goal attempt to the left with 1:06 remaining in the game at Ohio Stadium.

Buckeye fans let Harbaugh have it with obscene chants and nonstop venom, but he said it just served to get him and the team "jacked up" that much more.

"As I ran off," said Harbaugh, "I saw the smiling faces of my dad, mom, and family. That's something I'll never forget."

The emotions of the Harbaughs ran the entire gamut that week. Jack was fired as the head coach at Western Michigan, where his brother, John, was also part of the coaching staff that was dismissed. But the quarterback's father and brother both were beaming with pride and joy outside the team's locker room.

"I was thrilled for Jim," John said. "That guarantee quote was no surprise to me. People said it was out of character. But he wasn't cocky and was right in character. Ever since Jim was ten years old, he said he was going to take Michigan to the Rose Bowl."

Leach had been "Jimmy's" inspiration as a kid. He took Michigan to those three Rose Bowls he got to see from the sidelines and encouraged him …when he wasn't driven to taking the adhesive tape to him. Jim had a senior season pretty much identical to Leach's. Both finished third in Heisman voting, made All-American, were named the Big Ten's MVP, and led the Wolverines to the Big Ten championship and Pasadena.

"I'll tell you something about that," said Leach, "and I know Coach Harbaugh would tell you the same thing. I loved being their quarterback. I loved being their leader. I played in 48 straight games, and I always wanted my team to know they could count on me. And I think Coach Harbaugh was the same way.

"We both also had a respect that football games are won in the trenches. We both had a great offensive line and a great defensive line, and Jimmy and I also were blessed with great quarterbacks, receivers, and running backs with us. With the defenses we had, we knew we had a chance in every single game," Leach's point being that their victories, statistics, and awards were the result of being able to lead an exceptional team with exceptional coaches.

Harbaugh's guaranteed win over Ohio State, during which he threw for 261 yards and tailback Jamie Morris ran for 210 yards and two touchdowns, allowed Schembechler's credo to hold true: "Those Who Stay Will Be Champions."

The Wolverines would've fallen short of the Rose Bowl and Big Ten title had they lost. And for the first and only time, players who spent four years in Schembechler's program would have been denied the coveted conference championship and trip to Pasadena.

Michigan had an unusual schedule that season and also beat Hawaii in Honolulu on December 6 in a bowl game tune-up.

The Rose Bowl game against Arizona State started great for the Wolverines. Harbaugh completed a 24-yard pass to Greg McMurtry on the second play from scrimmage, and Morris capped the drive with an 18-yard touchdown run. Kicker Mike Gillette, a star high school quarterback, threw a pass to Gerald White for a two-point conversion. And by the time Harbaugh scored on a 2-yard run, Michigan led, 15–3. But they never scored again, getting shut out in the second half of a 22–15 loss to the Sun Devils.

A classic photo of Harbaugh and Schembechler on the sideline at the 1987 Rose Bowl, the coach with his left hand on his headset and the fingers of his right hand curled around the collar of his quarterback's jersey while he barked out the next play, takes up a place of honor in Harbaugh's coaching office at Schembechler Hall.

Bo signed it: "To Jim, a great quarterback…a good friend. Best Wishes, Bo Schembechler."

There is no photo that better captures the essence of Michigan football over the last half-century: The coach who changed everything and the quarterback who changed everything together in the Promised Land.

Coach Bo Schembechler tugs on quarterback Jim Harbaugh's jersey collar while shouting over the crowd and sending in a play in the 1987 Rose Bowl game with Arizona State.
*AP Photo/Reed Saxon.*

Part Three

# ART FOUR

## THE TRADITION CONTINUES

# Coach Gary Moeller

Gary Moeller packed a whole lot of winning and championships into his five seasons as the head coach at Michigan.

Moeller won three Big Ten titles, went 4–1 in bowl games while splitting a pair of Rose Bowls, and was 3–1–1 against Ohio State. He was 44–13–3 for a .758 winning percentage that just edged Lloyd Carr's .753.

And Moeller did something that none of the conference's coaching legends could match. His teams set the Big Ten record for most consecutive conference wins at 19 with powerhouse teams from 1990-92.

He's easily the most underrated coach in Wolverine history—especially when considering that he also spent eighteen years as an assistant coach under Schembechler and was highly successful as both a defensive and offensive coordinator.

Moeller's players knew just how special he was, though. He was not only an innovator but a coach who related to his players as individuals and was a superior recruiter. Moeller turned superstar tailback Tyrone Wheatley from Michigan State to Michigan during their sit-down talk on his recruiting visit.

"He was a guy who listened to me," said Wheatley. "Now, did I get my way? Maybe 2 percent of the time I did. But what was important was that he always listened. And in his responses to what I had to say, he had a way of painting a picture with his words for me with analogies and stories that he had of himself. For every situation I presented, he had a well-thought-out, articulate answer.

"That's my guy! He got it. I had admiration and true respect for him as a player and still do. We talk all the time."

Wheatley followed Moeller into coaching and became the running backs coach for the Jacksonville Jaguars in 2017 after two seasons as the Wolverines' running backs coach.

Jamie Morris, who rushed for 4,393 yards at Michigan and remained the career all-purpose yardage leader at 6,201 yards thirty years after playing his final game in 1987, watched Moeller operate as an ultra-successful defensive coordinator before becoming the offensive coordinator for his senior season.

What impressed Morris most about Moeller?

"His innovative mind," said Morris. "He was just constantly adding things to the offense. Mo was way ahead of his time. Mo was an offensive genius, and he was just so innovative that people couldn't keep up with him.

"Think about the players he brought here in a short amount of time. It was like, with Coach Mo, he was one of us. He played the game and knew what we were doing and what was going through your head."

Morris said Moeller convinced Schembechler, whom he also revered, to take him off the demonstration team as a freshman, when Morris rushed for 573 yards.

"Mo made the game so easy for us to understand," said Morris. "You just knew Gary Moeller was going to be the next coach after Bo. Gary Moeller set himself apart."

Gary Moeller (left) with Bo Schembechler, the Michigan athletic director and football coach, at the introductory press conference in 1989 when Moeller was named as Schembechler's replacement.
*Courtesy of Bentley Historical Library, University of Michigan.*

Moeller replaced Bo as head coach in 1990 and had five outstanding seasons before moving on to the NFL and completing his coaching career there. Carr, who had Moeller serve as the best man in his wedding, replaced him in 1995 and led the Wolverines to the 1997 national championship with a team sparked by Heisman Trophy winner Charles Woodson, a member of Moeller's last recruiting class.

And, as an assistant to Schembechler, Moeller was the primary recruiter of 1991 Heisman winner Desmond Howard, a running back from Cleveland St. Joseph whom Schembechler also loved. Moeller had to do a sell job on Bo to also offer a scholarship to Desmond's high school quarterback, Elvis Grbac. Schembechler wasn't sure if Grbac had the mobility he required in quarterbacks, but Moeller was convinced that he did after watching him play basketball.

Grbac set several passing records at Michigan, getting his start with Moeller as the offensive coordinator before becoming his head coach. Moeller installed a pro-style offense, and Michigan's goal-line offense went from the wishbone option under Schembechler to a slant-and-fade passing route combination. Grbac used his strong arm and feathery touch to connect with Howard and Derrick Alexander, both of whom became All-Americans and NFL first-round draft picks.

Moeller's teams had dynamic blockers as well as elite skill position players. Michigan's 1991 Gator Bowl MVPs after a dismantling of Ole Miss were center Steve Everitt, guards Dean Dingman and Matt Elliott, and tackles Greg Skrepenak and Tom Dohring—each of whom went on to the NFL.

Moeller was a two-way player at Ohio State, where his offensive line coach was Schembechler and his head coach was Woody Hayes. They all won a national championship together in 1961, and Moeller was a co-captain in 1962. He was a star linebacker but also played center and guard on offense.

"I always loved playing for linemen," said Everitt. "Knowing that [Moeller's] roots were playing center and O-line, that always took me to a place with him immediately.

"He was so knowledgeable about the game. He was just oozing with football knowledge. And, you know, you always hear about Coach Schembechler and Coach Carr, and I loved them both, and they deserve it. But I think Coach Moeller had a lot to offer, too."

Moeller had an insatiable desire for football knowledge.

He even took film with him on the family's annual summer vacation. He was good about going out on the pontoon boat, swimming with the kids, and grilling dinner. But when his family went away for a few hours, he pulled out the projector.

"I came back and found him stretched out on the floor there, watching film," said his wife, Ann. "He couldn't have been happier."

Moeller came to Michigan with Schembechler in 1969 as the defensive ends coach and considered being part of that season's epic upset of No. 1 Ohio State, the highlight of 23 seasons in Ann Arbor as either an assistant or head coach.

The January 1, 1993, Rose Bowl win over Washington was his most memorable game as head coach. Grbac's 15-yard touchdown pass to talented tight end Tony McGee secured that 38–31 victory.

Moeller also made his mark on defense as the coordinator from 1974 to 1976 and again from 1982 tö 1986. The Wolverines led the nation in scoring defense in three of those seasons: 1974 (6.8 points), 1976 (7.4), and 1985 (6.8).

That 1985 team had four All-Americans on defense either that year or in the next two seasons: defensive ends Mike Hammerstein and Mark Messner and cornerbacks Brad Cochran and Garland Rivers.

Linebacker Andy Moeller, his son, was the leading tackler with 68 solos, 46 assists, and 114 total. Mike Mallory, a linebacker and the also the son of a college football coach, was next with 101 tackles and as tough as nails.

Gary Moeller spent three seasons as the head coach at Illinois in between those defensive coordinator stints, going 6–24–3 from 1977 to 1979, and getting fired before receiving a complete opportunity to turn around a struggling program. He then spent two seasons as the Wolverines' quarterback coach to John Wangler and others before returning to defense, and he was the offensive coordinator for three seasons before becoming Michigan's head coach.

Jerry Hanlon coached at Miami of Ohio when Moeller was the freshman team coach for Schembechler in the mid-1960s. He watched Moeller mature as a coach and stayed on his staff for two seasons when Moeller replaced Schembechler.

"Gary is a very personable person," said Hanlon. "He's somebody you liked to be around. He was a good football player himself. He came from a football area, and football just seemed to be in his blood from the time he was born in Lima, Ohio."

Moeller grew up there with Ann and her brother, Joe Morrison, who went on to star for the New York Giants and become a successful college coach at South Carolina. Football did seem to be everywhere Moeller turned, and his son, Andy, ended up being a longtime coach and was a member of John Harbaugh's staff when the Baltimore Ravens won Super Bowl XLVII.

Gary Moeller coached many position groups—defensive ends, quarterbacks, tight ends, and linebackers—in addition to coordinating on both sides of the ball and serving as a head coach. He was 4–3 as the interim coach of the Detroit Lions in 2000. But what he did best was coach people, and appeal to his players on a personal level.

"The most important relationship you have as a coach is how you get along with the kids that you coach," said Hanlon, "and Gary Moeller surely fit that mold of a coach who built strong relationships with his players."

Moeller said the greatest thing he earned from Schembechler "was watching him handle players" and relate to them. He enjoyed that as much or more than watching film, coaching technique, forming game plans, or making calls in games.

Moeller was passionate about every element of coaching, and it showed in results that went beyond the won-loss record.

"Gary was, through-and-through, a man of the players," said Wolverine quarterback Brian Griese. "He was there for the players and genuinely cared how his players were doing not only on the field but off the field."

And that is quite a legacy.

# Elvis to Desmond: Fourth-Down Magic Against Notre Dame

It's called "The Catch," and the fourth-down completion for a 25-yard touchdown from Elvis Grbac to Desmond Howard in the fourth quarter against Notre Dame on September 14, 1991, was a true classic that's been savored ever since. It was the gutsiest and best-executed pass play the Wolverines have ever had in a big game.

As Grbac barked out his signals at the line, legendary announcer Brent Musburger intoned over the roar of the crowd: "Fourth and a foot."

Surely, the ball would go to tailback Ricky Powers, who ended up with 38 carries for 164 yards and one touchdown in that game against the Fighting Irish. And if not Powers, then fullback Burnie Legette, right?

Notre Dame's defense definitely thought a run up the gut was coming and stacked the line in every attempt to clog each running lane.

However, as Grbac dropped back to pass, Powers drifted to the left and was wide-open for a short pass. Legette ran to the right to block.

Grbac was going for all the marbles. He dropped back and pumped his arm to pass downfield. The pump froze two Irish defensive backs converging on Howard as he sprinted to the right corner of the end zone.

"They went for it all!" said TV analyst Dick Vermeil, the former UCLA and NFL coach.

Howard raced behind the cornerback and the safety was too late. He dove into the back of the end zone, caught the ball over his shoulder while in full flight with both hands outstretched, and cradled it into his gut while crashing to the ground.

"A diving catch for a touchdown!" shouted Musburger. "Holy cow! Would you believe this?"

What Vermeil couldn't believe was Michigan coach Gary Moeller's derring-do.

"You talk about a guts decision call by a coach!" exclaimed Vermeil. "I wouldn't have the guts to make the call."

To begin with, it was fourth down. J. D. Carlson, a money kicker, could have nailed a 42-yard field goal to make it a six-point lead with 9:02 remaining. Instead, Moeller decided to go for the first down. That was a tough call by itself.

Then, to go deep … well, that was a whole other category of guts.

The ABC-TV director alertly audibled to his studio in New York, where Bo Schembechler, only two years removed from coaching the Wolverines, was working as an analyst.

Schembechler was wearing that Cheshire Cat grin of his.

He chuckled and said, "That was a great call by Coach Moeller. Every time I called it, it was incomplete."

The best follow-up question would've been: "Bo, did you *ever* throw on fourth down?"

Grbac was a master at putting touch on the ball, and he dropped it into Howard's waiting hands as if throwing to a basket. Grbac jumped up upon realizing it was indeed a touchdown and sprinted toward the end zone while pumping both fists over his head.

Desmond Howard fully extends to reach out and grab a fourth-down touchdown pass from Elvis Grbac, the big play of a win over Notre Dame at Michigan Stadium in 1991.
*Photo by Robert Kalmbach.*
*Courtesy of Bentley Historical Library, University of Michigan.*

Part Four

Howard was lofted from under both armpits by a charging lineman and was soon engulfed by the entire offensive line that included two-time All-America tackle Greg Skrepenak.

The quarterback and receiver jogged back toward the bench together, and they stopped briefly. Grbac pulled Howard, whom he played both football and basketball with at Cleveland St. Joseph, in tight and their facemasks bumped while they exchanged congratulations and elation. Their parents, sitting next to one another at Michigan Stadium just as they did at high school games, celebrated together.

While Carlson was adding the point-after kick, Musburger offered a play on the Notre Dame claim on good fortune being their destiny:

"For one time," Musburger said, "you've got to believe in the luck of the Wolverines."

That made it 24–14, and the scoring was over as Michigan shut down Notre Dame's All-America quarterback Rick Mirer and running back Jerome Bettis, both of whom Schembechler had once recruited heavily.

However, there was no "luck" in what No. 3 Michigan did to the No. 7-ranked Irish over the course of 60 minutes with a balanced running and passing attack. Their defense, led by Butkus Award winner Erick Anderson, also stepped up big. The Wolverines had a staggering 40:40 in time of possession while Notre Dame was held to its lowest scoring total in six years under Coach Lou Holtz.

Grbac completed an amazing 20-of-22 passes for 195 yards and that one touchdown. He was on his way to leading the NCAA in passing efficiency, and would do so again as a senior in 1992 before going on to a successful NFL career with the San Francisco 49ers, Kansas City Chiefs, and Baltimore Ravens.

Howard, coming off a four-touchdown game at Boston College, also ran for a 29-yard touchdown and caught six passes for 74 yards against the Irish. He landed on the cover of *Sports Illustrated* the next week for his heroics and became the front-runner for the Heisman Trophy he won in a landslide vote after setting a Big Ten record that still stands with 19 receiving touchdowns that season.

"There's no doubt that catch made me a candidate for the Heisman," Howard said before the Rose Bowl game four months later. "I didn't think much about anything but catching the ball at the time it happened, but when I went home that night and watched it on TV, I could see how spectacular it was."

Moeller said: "He [Desmond] just jukes the guy and takes off to the outside. As he went to do that and juked the guy, Elvis saw what was happening and saw him take off, and he just laid it up there. He did a great job throwing it with a lot of height on the ball so Desmond could adjust to it."

Grbac believed he'd overthrown Howard and blown the opportunity.

"When it left my hand it was kind of wobbly," Grbac said. "Dez was running as hard as he could and the ball was just floating."

But Howard, nicknamed "Magic" back in high school, floated with the ball to pluck it from the sky for all the glory and the game.

Moeller summed it up perfectly:

"When it works, it takes a guy like Elvis to throw it, a guy like Desmond to make it work and make me look smart.

"That was a good player making a great play. And that was very special, all the particulars. Some of those things kind of get away from you, but to have Elvis and Desmond do that in that situation against that team, with all the pressure of that game, was very, very special."

## Desmond Howard, 1991 Heisman Trophy Winner

Desmond Howard wasn't a player who the major college powers were beating down the door to sign. In today's recruiting vernacular, he would've likely been rated a three-star recruit, somebody with good potential. But no overnight fan club formed in Ann Arbor when he chose to come to Michigan.

Howard didn't play as a freshman in 1988, but he developed quickly in practices, and Coach Bo Schembechler fell in love with the game-breaking qualities the former Cleveland St. Joseph High tailback possessed.

That became clear in the steamy coaches' room in Ohio Stadium after receiver-returner John Kolesar went 100 yards on two plays, a kickoff return and touchdown catch, to beat Ohio State in the final two minutes of a great game in The Horseshoe. I nicknamed Kolesar "The Buckeye Killer" because he had a real knack of making big plays against the team from his home state, and I asked Schembechler what he was going to do in this game without Kolesar next year.

Schembechler, his body still red from the hot shower, cracked a smile that lit up his face and said, "I've got a feisty little devil to take his place named Desmond Howard. Wait until you see him!"

Still, things didn't go as planned immediately. Howard was spinning his wheels on a very talented roster, trying to make his mark on teams that began a string of five consecutive Big Ten championships the year he arrived in Ann Arbor.

That's where Greg Harden, currently the Director of Athletic Counseling and an Associate Athletic Director at Michigan, entered his story and helped guide him to greatness.

"His gift is what he does," Howard said of Harden in 2017. "It's like Prince. People said his greatest gift was his musical genius. He could play every instrument at a high level, was a talented singer, and what he was doing was his gift.

"And to me, Greg's gift is to listen and analyze, to break down, to communicate, to share philosophy theories, and all of that to any individual sitting before him. That is his gift."

One that keeps giving.

"He's a rare, rare gem," said Howard. "I've always said he's our secret weapon and that Michigan is very fortunate to have him."

Howard said he wouldn't have developed into a Heisman Trophy winner without Harden, who remains one of his closest friends.

According to Harden, "Desmond was the first athlete that I had ever met who said, 'I want you to teach me everything about what you are talking about.' I mean this kid is eighteen or nineteen and decides that makes total sense."

His teaching begins with "identifying self-defeating attitudes and behaviors" of others.

"And they supply me a list of things that will sabotage a person's dreams," said Harden. "That puts it in the proper context for them, and it's no longer somebody telling them: 'Don't do this and don't do that.'

"What I am trying to teach them is to become the world's greatest expert on you—what works and doesn't work, what gets you closer to your dream and what sabotages it."

Howard became a master of that discipline.

"Desmond's mission was to become the best athlete on the team," said Harden. "His mission was not the Heisman but to become so comfortable being him that everything he did he would do better than the average person."

Howard said that when he came to Michigan in 1988, each football player was required to meet with Harden, who had made a great impression on Schembechler to gain his entry into working with the Wolverines, first with football players and then with those on all thirty-one athletic teams.

"I was so impressed by him, his delivery and his information," said Howard. "He could hold your attention for forty-five or fifty minutes and you wouldn't even get restless.

"Today, we're still friends, and I still learn from Greg. He is the sounding board for everything I've gone through and continue to go through. But at that age, when I was at Michigan, Greg Harden helped me see the big picture. There was a whole big world beside the bubble that you currently reside in as a student-athlete, and not to let that term define you."

The future Heisman winner needed to develop resolve and belief in himself before he could assert himself at Michigan.

Howard showed flashes in 1989, but he couldn't break into the starting lineup with future NFL receivers Greg McMurtry, who had been a highly publicized recruit, and Chris Calloway in front of him.

It wasn't until 1990 that Howard became a starter in his third season in the program, teaming with the fleet Derrick Alexander to wreak havoc with quarterback Elvis Grbac, his teammate at Cleveland St. Joe who also was lightly recruited but broke nearly every passing record at Michigan.

Howard and Alexander, from Detroit Benedictine, were fabulous high school basketball players who could also hold court on a grass field that measured 100 yards. Grbac had a strong, accurate arm and, most importantly, great touch. I'm convinced he could've thrown balls into a bushel basket 50 yards downfield.

This trio—blessed with one of the finest offensive lines in school history and a bevy of talented running backs to keep defenses honest—launched Michigan into the forefront as a passing attack.

Gary Moeller replaced the retired Schembechler that year, scrapped the option attack for a pro-style offense, and worked with assistant coach Cam Cameron and others to change the face of Wolverines offensive football.

Gone, too, was the wishbone option Schembechler favored in short-yardage and goal-line situations.

Moeller replaced that with Howard and Alexander running slant and fade routes on the same pass play. Grbac would either drop it into one of them in the corner of the end zone or throw a dart to the other cutting across the goal line.

They were lethal and beautiful, a football ballet.

Howard caught 63 passes for 1,025 yards and 11 touchdowns that season, leading the Big Ten in all three of those categories. His performance against Ole Miss in the Gator Bowl—where he averaged 26.6 yards on six catches and one run to net two touchdowns—got him into the conversation for the next season's Heisman.

Two games into the season, Howard was on his way to becoming the runaway Heisman winner. He scored four touchdowns in the opener at Boston College, including a 93-yard kickoff return and three catches, and then scored a dramatic, fourth-down touchdown on a 25-yard pass from Grbac against Notre Dame that landed him on the cover of *Sports Illustrated*.

Howard caught 62 passes for 985 yards and a Big Ten-record 19 touchdowns in 1991.

He scored 23 touchdowns, averaging a shade over two per game, to tie San Diego State tailback Marshall Faulk for the NCAA lead.

His signature scoring play, and the final one of his college career, was the 93-yard punt return touchdown that finished off Ohio State and sent the Wolverines to the Rose Bowl as Big Ten champions.

The "feisty little devil" comment had come full circle, with Howard sticking it to the Buckeyes with all the dramatic flair of Kolesar and more.

The Heisman pose Howard struck in the end zone on that overcast November afternoon has become the most replayed play any Wolverine has produced.

So the kid who came in with little fanfare departed as the darling of college football.

Wolverines receiver Desmond Howard poses with the Heisman Trophy at the Downtown Athletic Club in New York on December 14, 1991.
*AP Photo/Mark Lennihan.*

The stories of such players are fascinating because they had so much to overcome in getting to the top.

How, exactly, did Howard make that happen?

His path to greatness began with the counsel of two great parents, J. D. Howard and Hattie Dawkins, and with a decision he made to make the sacrifices necessary to attend Cleveland St. Joe, a school on the shores of Lake Erie which had a tremendous academic and athletic reputation. And before that, it began with his choice of teams in middle school.

Howard drove his bike with the banana seat two miles each way down some mean streets to practice each night with St. Tim's, a CYO team for eighth-and ninth-graders.

"I could have just walked down the street and played with another team," according to Howard. "But I wanted to play for the best, and St. Tim's was the Michigan of the Pee Wee leagues."

Choosing a challenge over convenience continued in high school. John F. Kennedy High was a short walk from his home, but he rode two hours each morning on a series of buses to reach St. Joe, a Catholic prep school.

Howard always took the long road, the one less traveled. And as poet Robert Frost once wrote, that made all the difference.

"I learned the value of sacrifice," Howard said. "I had to cut loose friends to go to St. Joe's and wake up at 5:30 a.m. You have to sacrifice to be the best and have a plan."

From a young age, he had a plan.

That plan was simple: attain greatness.

And he wouldn't let anything get in the way of doing that.

"If Desmond had two broken legs," his mother said then, "he would find a way to climb to the mountaintop."

Howard was appreciative that his parents, though no longer married, came together so often for him because of football. They openly praised one another for the job each did with him when I spent a full day with both of them shortly before their son won the Heisman.

"Coming from a family that breaks up does not dictate that you will become a juvenile delinquent," Howard said. "J. D. and my mother both stressed that you must take responsibility for yourself."

They also sacrificed to allow Desmond and his three brothers the opportunities to succeed.

"I owe everything to both of them," Desmond said. "I get my humanitarian qualities from my mom. My love of children came from working with her daycare kids. The competitiveness comes from my father. J. D. is an extremist—a competitor who believes you finish what you start."

J. D. lights up a room when he enters; he makes others smile more quickly than even his son can. But he also has a fire inside.

Desmond is very much a reflection of both of them.

Howard got his degree from Michigan five months after winning the Heisman, graduating in less than four years. He left for the NFL with a year of eligibility remaining, having nothing left to prove as a college player with a degree in hand.

He was the fourth overall pick in the first round by the Washington Redskins and was a great kick returner but a nondescript receiver during 11 pro seasons. However, he was named MVP of Super Bowl XXXI for sparking the Green Bay Packers' victory over the New England Patriots by returning a kickoff 99 yards for a touchdown and tying a Super Bowl record with 244 return yards.

He became a popular announcer on ESPN's College GameDay after retiring as a player and lives in Miami with his family.

Life's been good for Howard, who's found a way to succeed at every turn.

## Tyrone Wheatley's Rose Bowl Romp

Tyrone Wheatley ran like a runaway train in the 1993 Rose Bowl. There was no stopping him on three touchdown runs that totaled 168 yards—an amazing display, especially when considering that he was running hurt on two of them.

He rushed for 4,178 yards in a marvelous college career, and the 235 yards he gained on only 15 carries in Michigan's 38–31 win over Washington was the most Wheatley gained in one game.

It was a performance to cherish, and those touchdowns were his signature runs.

Wheatley scored first on a spirited 56-yard run that fired up Michigan and provided a 10-point lead.

Next up was the 88-yard touchdown run that showed why Wheatley also was an All-American and Big Ten champion sprinter in track and field.

Tenacious center Steve Everitt threw the block that sprang Wheatley near the line of scrimmage. Then it was off to the races for Wheatley, breezing down the middle of the field. Two safeties, the last defenders with a chance, had angles on him. But they didn't have Wheatley's speed, and he blew through them as if they weren't there.

"I remember seeing the back of Tyrone's jersey a lot," said Everitt. "Nothing like throwing a pancake [block] and seeing Tyrone run past me.

Tyrone Wheatley scores on 56-yard run in the 1993 Rose Bowl. He sparked the Wolverines to a win over Washington despite battling injuries.
*AP Photo/Bob Galbraith.*

"He was a beast. He was a big guy [6-foot, 235 pounds], and all he needed was a little crack. Not many guys could run with Tyrone. It was fun to block for him, fun to play with him. He was legitimate. He was a tough guy."

The 24-yard touchdown, though the shortest of his three touchdowns, might have been the most impressive because Wheatley had lost feeling in his left leg.

"I hurt my back early in the second quarter," Wheatley said. "And as the game progressed, it just got worse. On the last run, the left leg was numb. I remember telling myself on that one, 'Just run, just run, just run.' It was funny because my high school track coach asked me why I was struggling and didn't look smooth. I said, 'I couldn't feel my leg! I was just trying to get to the end zone.'"

Wheatley bumped the draw play outside to the right and could smell pay dirt. He dragged safety Tommie Smith into the end zone. But the game had taken its toll on his body, and the touchdown with 1:48 remaining in the third quarter was his last play.

He set Michigan's bowl rushing record—nipping by one yard the 234-yard effort of Jamie Morris in the 1988 Hall of Fame Bowl in Tampa against Alabama—to finish with 1,357 yards in 1992, when he was the Big Ten's Offensive Player of the Year.

"That was my favorite run of the game," Wheatley said of his 15th and final carry. "I just remember looking in all the guys' faces, and we were tired. They were tired. It was a heavyweight fight, and we were slugging it out. Everyone was bruised and battered.

"I stiff-armed a guy, and after I stiff-armed him it propelled me, and I got my foot off the ground. Once I saw the open field, it was usually, 'Put up six points and strike up the band.' On this one, it was, 'Oh, God, I hope I make it.'

"And when I did, I jumped up and celebrated. People said, 'If your leg was numb, how did you jump up?' But I'd made it, and I knew our defense would do what it had to do."

Michigan held the Huskies scoreless in the fourth quarter.

Ed Davis picked up some critical yards for the Wolverines in the final quarter, and quarterback Elvis Grbac's 15-yard touchdown pass to tight end Tony McGee with 5:29 remaining put Michigan ahead for good.

Choosing the MVP was decided much earlier.

The 15.7 yards Wheatley averaged in that game also remains the highest per-carry total by any Wolverine with at least 15 carries in one game. There were only six games in the first 138 years of Michigan football in which a runner topped his 235.

"It was the prototypical stars and the moon aligning perfectly," said Wheatley. "My offensive line was blocking incredibly along with receivers like Derrick Alexander and Amani Toomer and those guys.

"That was the best-blocked game that I've ever been a part of."

Wheatley also credited Grbac, who was playing his last game and finished his career as Michigan's career leader in passing yardage and touchdowns. Washington had beaten the Wolverines in the previous Rose Bowl, and Grbac wouldn't allow a repeat.

"Just like he led the band in 'The Victors' after the game," said Wheatley, "Elvis was our orchestrator. He had been on teams that played and fought and lost in Rose Bowls. He understood what it took to become champions. He was the end of the Bo Schembechler era and brought that in along with Gary Moeller.

"Grbac was able to help young guys like myself understand that this was going to be tough and how to fight through hard times and manage games. He was a great leader for us in my first two years."

Washington had beaten Michigan, 34–14, in the previous Rose Bowl.

"Deep down, that was a huge factor," said Wheatley. "It was redemption. We wanted to prove that what we did the previous year wasn't really our team. We had underestimated them the year before and they played great.

"But in the next Rose Bowl, we just kept beating the proverbial drum and outlasted them. As many stars as we had, they had just as many. It was a great matchup. They were our equivalent. They had the same firepower we had."

Wheatley, surprisingly, said he'd never watched that Rose Bowl with his wife or five children in the quarter century that followed.

"No," he said. "I don't watch much of that with my kids. But when De'Anthony Thomas of Oregon broke my record for the longest Rose Bowl run (with a 91-yarder in the 2012 game), I was upstairs in the bed asleep, and my middle son, Terius, came up and said, 'You mean you had a run in the Rose Bowl that was a record that stood for 20 years?'

"He said, 'Dad, you're not watching this? He broke your record!' I said, 'Records are meant to be broken, son.' I went back to bed, and he was shaking his head."

Wheatley and his oldest son, Tyrone Jr., both came back to Ann Arbor in 2015, Jim Harbaugh's first season as the head coach. The son—a big, fast tight end—loved spending two years with his father, the running backs coach. Dad moved on to the Jacksonville Jaguars in 2017, where he coached the running backs during a turnaround season that saw that franchise return to the NFL postseason.

Wheatley, a first-round pick by the New York Giants who later played in the Super Bowl, accomplished much as a player and coach. But there's no debate about his single greatest game. It came in Pasadena on day when there was no stopping that runaway train wearing a winged helmet.

## Coach Lloyd Carr

Lloyd Carr was a college quarterback who coached defense exclusively in college, and that background provided him a pretty keen insight into what was happening on both sides of the line of scrimmage.

However, he was so much more than just a football coach. Carr could keep pace with most English professors in regard to having a long reading list, is a great family man, and consistently displays his deep compassion for others.

The pediatric cancer wing at the University of Michigan's Mott Children's Hospital is named the Coach Carr Unit and is where his young grandson, Chad, was treated before succumbing to a rare form of pediatric brain cancer in 2015.

Carr influenced his players in making weekly trips to Mott decades before it became a personal cause and accomplished so much beyond winning the 1997 national championship, which will always be his greatest legacy to most fans.

His players absolutely revere him and have followed his example in giving back. Brian Griese, Steve Hutchinson, and Charles Woodson—all starters on the '97 team who went on to NFL stardom—raised millions of dollars for Mott with their annual Champions for Children's Hearts Weekend that featured golf, celebrity galas, and radiothons.

"I try to parent my kids the way he shepherded us," said Griese. "I mean, every guy has been touched by him, even to this day. We try to emulate him with the way we live our lives—with the values and the ethics that we live our lives by.

"It's hard to measure his impact because his legacy lives on in my kids, and I don't think his legacy will ever die. The kind of person he was off the field is even more impressive than his accomplishments on the field."

Carr knew how to spread love, but used another form of it on the field—tough love.

"Lloyd's biggest thing was that he didn't care if you liked him, so to speak," said Braylon Edwards, the Biletnikoff Award winner as the nation's top receiver in 2004. "He wanted you to like him, but he only cared about bringing the best out of you. He was a master of turning you into a man and bringing that best out of you. He knew what buttons to touch to make you a better player or pull back and not give you a compliment because your head might be getting too big.

"He knew when to give you whatever advice was needed and was a master at making men better from the day they stepped in the door until they left. After leaving Michigan, I was a better man for playing for Lloyd Carr."

Carr, in 13 seasons, 1995 to 2007, won 122 games and ranked below only Bo Schembechler (194) and Fielding H. Yost (165) on the school's victory list. He joined both of them in the College Football Hall of Fame in 2011.

The Wolverines won five Big Ten championships under his watch, going 20–8 against teams ranked in the Top 10, and producing one Heisman Trophy winner in Woodson and twenty All-Americas: defensive or offensive tackles Jason Horn, Will Carr, Glen Steele, Jon Jansen, Rob Renes, and Jake Long; offensive guard Steve Hutchinson; defensive or offensive ends Jerame Tuman, David Terrell, Marquis Walker, Bennie Joppru, Edwards, and LaMarr Woodley; linebackers Jarrett Irons and Larry Foote; and defensive or running backs Charles Woodson, Marlin Jackson, Chris Perry, Ernest Shazor, and Leon Hall.

He impacted each and every one of them—as well as hundreds of players you never heard of—in very meaningful ways.

"In my life," said Jansen, "whenever I'm challenged with a tough decision, whether it's in business, my personal life, or a decision I need to make about or for my kids, or discipline, I think back to Coach Carr. He was always honest. He was always thoughtful. He was always fair. And I think to myself, 'What would Coach do in this situation?' It really helps me sort through the different variables and things.

"His first reaction wasn't, 'You're off the team and will have nothing to do with Michigan football.' It was, 'Let's get all the facts. Let's get what the repercussions of what happened are. Then, let's take a look at the type of guy who did this. Is this a one-time mistake or a repeat offender?' Then he took all of that into account and came up with a fair punishment. And sometimes it wasn't just punishment for the offender. The senior class leadership would have to enforce what he said had to be done.

"That's the greatest impact he had on me."

Wide receiver Tai Streets caught two touchdown passes from Griese as a junior in Michigan's 1998 Rose Bowl win over Washington State that clinched a national championship and was team MVP as a senior. He went on to play for the San Francisco 49ers and Detroit Lions before becoming a coach.

Streets said Carr molded him.

"He taught me to become a man," said Streets, "on and off the field. I was a kid coming here out of high school, and the tough love is what you need. These kids nowadays don't have that all the time. So he taught me to become a man on and off the field with tough love. It was neat.

"I use the same thing. I coach basketball at my high school, and I have an AAU program. Charles Matthews (a forward who debuted for the Wolverines in 2017–18) played for me. It's Mean Streets, AAU in Chicago. So it's amazing what impact he had on me and still has on me. If I have any questions, I still call him to see what he would do."

Carr also had a knack for motivating his players—and sometimes from something as goofy as a pillow fight after the team movie before a big game.

"We left our doors open because we had to get back to our rooms for bed check," recalled Edwards. "Guys would hurry back and turn up the thermostat in your room so it felt like 106 degrees after the movie. Or they would steal your pillows.

"So, one night, Chris Perry turned my thermostat up and took my pillows. I knew he did it because he had too many pillows at the movie. So I'm knocking on his door pretending to do room check."

Edwards impersonated the voice of long-time running backs coach Fred Jackson and said he had something to talk about with Perry.

Perry opened his door at the Campus Inn, where the team spent Friday nights before home games.

"I busted him in the head with a pillow," Edwards said. "He tackled me in the hallway, and we had a pillow fight. But I forgot his room was right next to Lloyd's room. So, the next thing I know, there's Lloyd: 'Damn it! Get your asses in the room! What the hell is going on out here?'

"Now, fast-forwarding ahead to the next day, we're losing to Penn State with about seven minutes to play. Chris and I look at each other and say, 'We can't lose this game. Not after last night!'"

Edwards loves this story and that game.

"This is actually my favorite game," he said. "I like this game better than Michigan State [in 2004] because we got caught pillow-fighting the night before, then we're down (21–14 with 7:46 left to play in the fourth quarter) to Penn State and Larry Johnson in the year when he ran for 2,000 yards. We scored to take it to overtime, and then Chris scores the winning touchdown in overtime."

Perry scored on a 3-yard run in OT after Penn State settled for a field goal, making Michigan a 27–24 winner. Edwards caught a 3-yard touchdown pass from John Navarre to force overtime in that game played on October 12, 2002. His performance wasn't close to the three-touchdown catch, triple-overtime win over the Spartans as a senior, but it was special to Braylon.

"Man," said Edwards, "we gave ourselves the biggest hug after the game and said, 'We didn't have any choice in hell.' If we'd lost that game, we'd have gotten benched for that game or the next two games. But the pillow-fighters pulled it out."

Carr had a lasting legacy despite a head coaching appointment that brought with it no sense of permanency.

Michigan athletic director Joe Roberson made Carr the interim coach in the spring of 1995 after Penn State coach Joe Paterno suggested that as the most sensible move because it was such an awkward time for all involved. A replacement had to be named for Gary Moeller, who had resigned, but that decision was pushed back to after the season.

Roberson said Schembechler bristled over his consulting a coach from outside the Michigan family, but he believed in reaching out for advice both in and out of the program. He already was well aware that Schembechler believed deeply in Carr and simply desired other opinions.

It didn't take Roberson long to be won over by Carr. He saw other qualities "that would make him a true role model to his players," and that appealed to the athletic director. He began trading books with Carr, as both were avid readers. Roberson was startled to hear Carr playing classical music in his office.

Those Renaissance man qualities eventually won over Michigan president James Duderstadt, who didn't appreciate the power Bo Schembechler had while coaching and directing the athletic department or even after leaving the university all together. Duderstadt had cringed when Schembechler avoided any formal search for his replacement by simply naming Gary Moeller, his longtime assistant. Carr, at first, was viewed as nothing more than another Schembechler selection by the president. However, in traveling with the football team during that in-flux season of 1995, Duderstadt, according to Roberson, came to appreciate the same things in Carr that Roberson did.

Literature played a big part in the motivation Carr used with a Wolverine team that won a national championship in just his third season as the head coach.

He used *Into Thin Air* by Jon Krakauer as the motivational theme for the magical 1997 season. The book dealt with a Mount Everest disaster during which eight climbers were killed and several were stranded by an unexpected storm. Carr gave each player on the team a pickaxe as a symbol of the rugged climb they were making together, and he quoted *Into Thin Air* throughout the season.

When his team beat Washington State in the Rose Bowl to finish an undefeated season that resulted in the Associated Press poll's No. 1 ranking, Carr had the perfect, ready-made analogy to sum up their accomplishment.

Carr shouted to his players huddled in the locker room in Pasadena: "We went to the summit—we're there!"

Mount Everest served as motivation for a memorable season, while "The Law of the Jungle," a poem from Rudyard Kipling's *The Jungle Book,* was painted onto the wall of the defensive team meeting room and has remained there:

"For the strength of the Pack is the Wolf

And the strength of the Wolf is the Pack."

The message from both the mountain and the jungle were the same. It was all about a group of individuals playing together and for one another.

The hallmark of Carr's teams might very well have been their spirit, fire, and pure competitiveness. It was ironic that those qualities were never clearer than in his first and last games as head coach of the Wolverines.

Carr was the interim coach for his first game on August 26, 1995, and nobody knew if there would be a second season for the defensive coordinator who had been elevated to take the place of Moeller, his close friend.

The No. 14 Wolverines faced No. 17 Virginia in the Pigskin Classic at Michigan Stadium, and the first 47 minutes of Carr's head coaching career couldn't have started much worse. However, the last 13 minutes of that game couldn't have gone any better.

Michigan trailed, 17–0, with 12:55 remaining in the game.

Scott Dreisbach, a nineteen-year-old redshirt freshman making his collegiate debut, had thrown two costly interceptions and the booing got louder as that zero on the scoreboard became more and more of an eyesore to fans.

However, Carr had told Dreisbach that he was going with him all the way and stuck to his word rather than switching to redshirt sophomore Griese, whose college debut came later that season when Dreisbach was injured. Carr had played quarterback at Missouri and Northern Michigan, and he knew the importance of having the coach totally in your corner.

The starting quarterback definitely rewarded his coach by throwing for an amazing 236 yards in the fourth quarter and a school-record 372 yards in the air for the entire game.

Dreisbach got it all started by completing 41- and 43-yard passes to Mercury Hayes on a touchdown drive that culminated with a 2-yard scoring run by tailback Ed Davis.

Then Dreisbach hit Hayes for a 31-yard touchdown pass on an out route with 7:47 remaining. However, the Wolverines trailed, 17–12, because a missed point-after kick was followed by a missed two-point conversion play.

They would get one final chance with the ball 80 yards from the Virginia end zone and 2:35 remaining.

Dreisbach's mojo, though, appeared to vanish as quickly as it had appeared once the Wolverines reached the 15 yard line with 18 seconds remaining.

He overthrew tight end Jay Riemersma and wide receiver Amani Toomer on consecutive plays, and then for some bizarre reason threw a pass well short of the end zone to Tyrone Butterfield. Butterfield said he knocked it down rather than grab it and get tackled quickly because time would've run out.

So there was one more play on fourth down with four ticks remaining on the clock.

Dreisbach looked off primary receiver Toomer to the left and threw to Hayes in the right corner of the end zone. The pass had plenty of touch on it and dropped into the waiting arms of Hayes, who had beat future Pro Bowl cornerback Ronde Barber and the additional coverage help coming from safety Paul London.

The question was whether or not Hayes was in bounds, and replays showed he'd gotten his left foot down to confirm the referee's signal for a touchdown in the days before video replay.

Perhaps the wildest dog-pile the Big House had ever seen ensued:

Michigan 18, Virginia 17.

Lloyd Carr (right) with Virginia coach George Welsh before kickoff of Carr's first game as the interim head coach of the Wolverines on August 26, 1995. The Wolverines staged an amazing comeback victory in that game at Michigan Stadium.
*Photo by Robert Kalmbach.*
*Courtesy of Bentley Historical Library, University of Michigan.*

Carr said he might never have become the permanent head coach, a status that he was granted that year on November 13 with an 8–2 record, had the Wolverines not pulled out that one.

He'd had a magical first game after averting what appeared to be a disastrous debut.

Carr had a great ride that ended with him getting carried off the field of the Citrus Bowl in Orlando on New Year's Day 2008.

Michigan had let a 14-point lead in the third quarter get away, and trailed Florida, 35–31, with 2:30 to play in the game. However, quarterback Chad Henne rallied the troops with an 18-yard touchdown pass to Adrian Arrington to culminate a drive that lasted less than one minute. K. C. Lopata's 41-yard field goal sewed up a 41–35 victory.

Tim Tebow, who had won the Heisman Trophy in that 2007 season and won national championships the year before and year after, couldn't pull out a miracle finish, and the Wolverines got that happy ending for their coach.

"They were a hungry team," said Tebow. "They came out ready to fight."

Carr wanted to speak with Gators coach Urban Meyer after the game, and this is what Meyer said Carr told him: "Someday, you're going to retire, and your players are going to play as hard as my guys did."

Carr let the tears flow before and after his finale.

"I told them I loved them," Carr said of his players. "Every guy in that locker room from here on out will be my friend. That is one of the joys of coaching."

And that summed up what he was about: winning games and winning the lifelong loyalty of his players.

Carr was a straight shooter, and that's what made him such a tremendous recruiter. I was fortunate enough to literally go out on the road with him as National Letter of Intent signing day approached in 1990 and saw that firsthand.

He also had a remarkable ability to juggle all of the demands that come in the hectic world of big-time recruiting.

Carr was driving down Interstate-94 in Chicago during our travels and had a cup of coffee in his right hand and a large phone in his left hand that was pressed to his ear. He was steering with his knees and talking to a football department secretary about changing travel plans on a trip that knew no end. The changes in the player commitments brought about changes in travel.

I sat next to him in the rental car, and he requested that I hand him a pen so he could write down a phone number. But he was out of hands! So I laughed and offered to write it down for him, and he repeated the number for me.

We visited thirteen recruits in forty hours, flying, driving and sometimes running in order to catch planes. It turned out to be a revealing look inside the process of wooing blue-chip players. Some came like linebacker Steve Morrison and defensive lineman Gannon Dudlar from Brother Rice High, then located in Birmingham, Michigan. Some went elsewhere, like running back Jerome Bettis of Detroit Mackenzie to Notre Dame. Gritty receiver Walter Smith, Bettis's teammate, did choose the Wolverines.

Notre Dame coach Lou Holtz called Carr while we drove through Milwaukee one night and tried wooing him away as his defensive coordinator with the possibility of strong consideration as Holtz's eventual replacement.

Chuck Noll of the Pittsburgh Steelers once offered him a spot on his staff, too. When Carr called Schembechler to notify him of the NFL offer, Schembechler told Carr to sit tight and wait until he drove to his house to discuss the overture.

Carr said Schembechler convinced him with this point:

"You're not a pro coach! You're a college coach. You should be working with kids. That's a business in the NFL. This is about making an impact on kids' lives!"

Bo had Lloyd pegged perfectly, and the assistant has been forever thankful he took the head coach's advice. So are the players he coached. Decades later, they are thankful he was their mentor, taking some from college to the pros, but all from boys to men.

## Biakabutuka Runs Wild Past Buckeyes

Tshimanga Biakabutuka could very well have given the Wolverines a Heisman Trophy winner sandwiched in between Desmond Howard and Charles Woodson.

Biakabutuka (bee-OCK-ah-buh-too-kuh) totaled a school-record 1,818 yards rushing in 1995, when he ran wild against Ohio State with 37 carries for 313 yards and the touchdown run that ended up being the difference in a 31–23 upset.

"I never saw holes that big," Biakabutuka said after the game. "Anybody here could have run through those holes and gained all those yards.

"I thought the Notre Dame game two years ago was the greatest win I'd ever been part of, but this is the best. Ohio State was ranked No. 2 in the nation, people were saying Michigan wasn't Michigan anymore, and we proved them wrong."

Redemption was the theme of the game for the Wolverines. They were 8–3, while the undefeated Buckeyes were a national championship contender with the Heisman favorite. Michigan coach Lloyd Carr said Biakabutuka told him he wanted to prove he was the Big Ten's best running back in that game, and his teammates prodded "Touchdown Tim" leading up to the game.

"That day, he just saw the challenge," said Wolverines offensive tackle Jon Jansen. "There was a lot of hype about Eddie George, and, 'Was he going to win the Heisman?' So we're egging on Tshimanga (tuh-MONG-ah): 'Why does it have to be Eddie George? You might not win the Heisman, but you can have your moment today.'

"It became more of an individual matchup for him. He wanted to outperform Eddie George. And for the rest of our lives, we can say, 'Tshimanga Biakabutuka, on that day, beat the pants off of Eddie George.' I can say I was part of it. Jon Runyan and the rest of the guys on our line can say that, too. And the first thing we talk about when we get together today is that game."

Tackles Runyan and Jansen, guards Joe Marinaro and Zach Adami, and center Rod Payne did blow open some huge holes. But Biakabutuka also stiff-armed, broke tackles, juked defenders with his swivel hips, and displayed relentless determination.

Biakabutuka had 45 yards after two carries, 104 yards (George's exact total for the game in 21 carries) on five carries, and quite simply punished the Buckeyes.

When it was all over, Biakabutuka unbuckled his chin strap, removed his helmet, and raised it in his right hand while running onto the field, bounding and shouting for joy.

Biakabutuka's rushing total has only been topped once in the history of Michigan football. Ron Johnson had 31 carries for 347 yards and five touchdowns against Wisconsin in 1968.

"When you have performances like that," said Jansen, "you look back to the first ten games and ask, 'Why didn't we perform like that the other ten times? Why did it take us—whether it was Ohio State or winning for the seniors—to get motivated?' I've thought about it all these years and never came up with a good answer.

Tshimanga "Touchdown Tim" Biakabutuka on his way to another big run in rushing for 313 yards against Ohio State in 1995.
*Courtesy of Bentley Historical Library, University of Michigan.*

"But it was awesome. No doubt."

It was the same kind of stunning performance Howard (1991) and Woodson (1997) used in Ohio State games at Michigan Stadium to win Heismans. However, that award went to George in 1995. Biakabutuka finished eighth, also placing behind Northwestern tailback Darnell Autry, in a season in which the Big Ten had three rushers exceed 1,700 yards.

George ran for 1,927 yards on 49 more carries than Biakabutuka had, and George's 5.9 yards-per-carry was three-tenths of a yard less than Biakabutuka's. But George had 24 touchdowns to Biakabutuka's 12 and was much more valuable in the passing game.

Still, based on their performances in "The Game," it could be argued that Biakabutuka deserved the Heisman. But Michigan's mediocre record that season dragged him down, fair or not.

"It's the winning record," said Jansen, "and these awards are popularity contests. When you have a university that actively promotes a player, people get hit with more Eddie George than they do Tshimanga Biakabutuka. At Michigan, it's all about the team, and we didn't publicize individuals. We pumped up the team, and we were all OK with that.

"That's part of the reason that Eddie George won the Heisman."

Biakabutuka opted to leave after his junior year off that performance and did edge George in first-round selection placement, going No. 8 to the Carolina Panthers while George went No. 16 to the Houston Oilers, who later became the Tennessee Titans.

George ended up having an overwhelmingly better pro career, while Biakabutuka struggled with injuries. His football career ended on October 21, 2001, when, after rushing for 121 yards against the Washington Redskins, he was gang-tackled and his foot was mangled so grotesquely that it dangled from his leg. His tendons were torn apart.

However, Biakabutuka went on to success in the business world with a jewelry store and owned several fast-food chicken restaurants.

"I have a lot of cousins in Africa who do not have the chance to do something with their lives," Biakabutuka said prior to that Ohio State game. "When I'm tired and beat up, I think of them. They would do anything to have this chance. And my parents helped a lot, too. Mom said to respect others, and if you respect, you stay humble. You strive to get better if you're humble because you never feel you're too good. Dad says be strong and believe you can do whatever anybody can."

Biakabutuka was born in Kinshasa, Zaire—which became known as the Democratic Republic of the Congo—in 1974, nine months before Muhammad Ali beat George Foreman in a highly publicized heavyweight title fight in his capital city hometown.

Six years later, his father, Mulenga Wa Biakabutuka, moved the family to study at the University of Montreal and became a teacher on a Cree Indian Reservation in the wilds of Quebec, returning to visit his family when he could. His mother, Misenga Batuabile Bibi, designed clothes.

I visited their home in Longueuil, just across the St. Lawrence River from Montreal, to detail their family story and discover the origins of an unlikely football talent.

Serge Benoit, his coach at Jacques Rousseau High in Montreal, discovered Biakabutuka when he was fifteen. "I noticed his athletic ability," Benoit said, "and asked, 'Why don't you play football?' He looked at me and said, 'If I play, I want to go far.' He was an aggressive character but easy to coach."

Still, if another Montreal coach, Marc Santere, hadn't taken Biakabutuka and others to the Michigan football camp in the summer of 1992, he very likely never would've become a Wolverine, and one of the greatest performances in school history might never have happened.

But it all happened to complete a story that proved, once again, fact can be stranger than fiction.

## Revisiting the 1997 National Champions

I (Derek) had the chance to meet with several members of one of Michigan football's most celebrated teams during their twentieth anniversary reunion held at Crisler Center in April of 2017. I was overcome with nostalgia watching so many of my boyhood heroes walk through the tunnel and into the arena. Some of them looked as if they could still throw on some pads and lead the maize and blue to another title, and some of them looked like the guy in front of you at a Chinese buffet. Some of them had full heads of hair, and some of them didn't have much lettuce left. But to a man, each one had a smile on his face as wide as the Grand Canyon. They were home. They were back with *The Team*.

Brian Griese, the starting quarterback and one of the leaders of that 1997 squad, recalled a moment during the very first team meeting that fall when all of the guys were gathered in the theater-style seating of the team meeting room at Schembechler Hall. He said that seniors always sat up front and that on that day there were two players who'd both had the same idea about which seat they were going to lay claim to for that season's meetings, and it was one of the much-coveted aisle seats in the first row. The two men involved in the dispute were senior fullback Chris Floyd and senior defensive lineman Ben Huff (the latter sadly passed away in 2006 at the age of thirty-one). As Griese put it, "Neither one of those guys were guys you wanted to mess with." He added, "Everybody in the room just kind of stopped, and we didn't know if they were gonna get into a fight or what was gonna happen." Now it goes without saying that if the very first team meeting of the season had kicked off with a fight between senior teammates it would have been a disaster for any college football team going forward. But what happened next may just have set the tone for what this team went on to accomplish at the end of the season. Griese said that at the exact same instant, Floyd and Huff both took a step back, took a breath, and decided that they weren't going to fight about a seat. "They checked their egos at the door, and we became a team. Everybody watched that and said, you know what, we're not gonna fight each other, we're gonna love each other, and we're gonna do this together."

Michigan was coming off of four straight four-loss seasons, so expectations weren't exactly sky high before their 1997 season opener at home against Colorado, which had broken the hearts of 106,000-plus at Michigan Stadium just three years earlier in the most dramatic and brutal fashion with Kordell Stewart's "Hail Mary" touchdown pass. Michigan would have its revenge that day, though, taking away any lingering heartache from '94 by trouncing the Buffaloes, 27–3. It was more of the same the next week when the Baylor Bears came to town, and the following week they beat a very good Notre Dame team in the Big House, 21–14. At this point, Wolverine faithful were starting to get an inkling that this team might be capable of making a run at the Big Ten title. Dominant wins in the following two weeks over Indiana and Northwestern further fueled growing expectations around Ann Arbor and set up yet another home game for the 5–0 Wolverines against the 4–1 Iowa Hawkeyes who'd just lost convincingly to Ohio State the previous Saturday, 23–7.

Michigan came out flat in the first half and found themselves trailing the Hawkeyes, 21–7, at halftime and you could almost hear the collective thoughts of Wolverine nation all thinking to themselves, *If we're down 21–7 at the half and Ohio State beat this team 23–7 last week...* But the mood inside the Michigan locker room at the half that Saturday was far more calm and optimistic. I spoke with defensive lineman Glen Steele at the reunion about the resolve that the team showed that day, and he said, "Coach Carr walks in [the locker room at the half], doesn't say anything. Guys walk in but there was no fatigue, there wasn't any worry. It was just, OK, how are we gonna fix this? At the end of the day we had to get one more point than these guys. There was no panic, there was nothing like that. We had great leadership."

Taking cues from their head coach and senior leadership, the Wolverines came out and played an inspired second half. With the defense holding the Hawkeyes offense to just three points in the entire half, it enabled the Michigan offense to put up 21 to secure a 28–24 victory. Griese had three interceptions in the first half but told the team he had never played worse in a half. Then he calmly added that he was going to play his best half, and his teammates picked up on his confidence. The senior quarterback threw for two touchdowns and ran for another.

The team had faced their first hiccup half of the season and figured out a way to make the proper corrections and adjustments to get the win, and any championship team will tell you that there's almost always that one game where they came out flat early or midway through the season and they figured out a way to pull it out. As Michigan Stadium held its breath during the first half, a confident Wolverine football team navigated the adversity and got themselves out of a corner and into the Big Ten title and national championship conversation.

The following week, Michigan travelled 70 miles north to face a 5–1, Nick Saban-led Michigan State team. The game itself does not stand out years later as a particularly interesting meeting between the in-state rivals (Michigan won convincingly, 23–7), but what is etched indelibly on the minds of all Wolverine fans who witnessed it is the unbelievable interception that Charles Woodson made on the sideline in that game. Woodson glided across an overcast Michigan sky, right arm outstretched, and plucked a 3rd-and-nine pass that had to have been at least 13 feet in the air out of that gray sky, and when his left foot came back to earth in bounds, the entire college football world knew his name. It was his first step towards the Downtown Athletic Club in New York.

The game at home the next week provided another showcasing of just how good the Michigan defense was that season. Holding Minnesota to just three points set the tone for the extremely tall task the unbeaten Wolverines were going to face in their final three games of the regular season … away to Penn State, away to Wisconsin, and then back home to host Ohio State in "The Game" and the maize and blue's first shot at an undefeated season, without a tie, since 1948.

Going into the ballgame in Happy Valley, the polls had the Nittany Lions sitting at No. 2 and the Wolverines sitting at No. 4. This matchup with definite Big Ten and national title implications had the college football world salivating.

Between the two teams, there were forty-six players who dressed that day who would go on to play in the NFL. Penn State was having a season that had their fans tasting a national championship, but that Saturday, the Wolverines quickly slapped that taste out of their mouths. From the get-go, it was never really even a contest. Michigan was the tougher, more physical team right out of the gates. And with a 10–0 lead, on the last play of the first quarter, Daydrion Taylor put a hit on Penn State tight end Bob Stephenson that sent a hush around Beaver Stadium. In an interview for the Big Ten Network in 2012, Charles Woodson said, "It's gotta be the hardest hit I've ever witnessed." Neither team knew it that day, but that hit would end both players' football careers. It did, however, serve as fuel for the Michigan defense for the rest of that season. Twenty years later, linebacker Sam Sword recalled the effect that the hit had, saying, "We put our foot on the gas a little bit more, because you never know when it's gonna be your last game."

After witnessing a season-ending injury of a teammate, average teams tend to shrink and look for ways to avoid contact. Championship teams turn it up a notch and go as hard as they can for their fallen brother.

Michigan was as dominant in the next three quarters as they were in the first, dismantling the Nittany Lions for a 34–8 final score, leaving very little doubt in the minds of the Associated Press poll voters as to who was the best team in the country.

Camp Randall Stadium in Madison, Wisconsin, was everything you'd expect it to be on November 15 for a matchup against Michigan, now ranked No. 1. It was filled to capacity, there was newly fallen snow plowed to the edges of the field, and Barry Alvarez had his No. 24 Badgers ready to play spoiler to the Wolverines' perfect season. The only thing missing that day was the injured Wisconsin running back, Ron Dayne. Without Dayne, Wisconsin struggled to get much of anything going offensively. Michigan dominated both sides of the ball in the first half, with an outstanding effort by committee from the backfield of Chris Howard, Anthony Thomas, and Chris Floyd. They may have gotten caught looking ahead to the next game a little bit in the second half but escaped Madison with a 26–16 win. The stage was set for one of the biggest games to ever take place in Michigan Stadium.

There was electricity in the air on November 22, 1997, at Michigan Stadium and a level of confidence about that game within the stadium that was palpable to both the players and the fans. This was what every Michigan player and fan dreamed about. One more win against their biggest rivals and the Wolverines would be going to Pasadena to play for a national championship.

Every great team needs to have a truly great player, someone who's the best on the field every time he walks out of the tunnel. A player who sets the tone in every game he plays in. Charles Woodson knew he was that player, and so did Ohio State. Michigan's 20–14 victory that day was certainly a team effort, but I think that it's safe to say that without Woodson, that game may have had a very different outcome. He returned a punt 78 yards for a touchdown, set up a touchdown with a 37-yard reception, and intercepted a pass in the Michigan end zone.

Charles Woodson sprints down the left sideline on his 78-yard punt return touchdown against Ohio State in 1997. This run and his superb all-around game against the Buckeyes helped Woodson claim the Heisman Trophy.
*Photo by Sara Stillman.*
*Courtesy of Bentley Historical Library, University of Michigan.*

The college football world recognized the same in Woodson in the weeks to follow, awarding him the Heisman Trophy. He was the first, and to this day, only primarily defensive player to ever win it. So with Heisman in hand and an undefeated, battle-tested team behind him, Charles and the Wolverines headed to Southern California for their shot at immortality.

Sitting in the stands that day at the Rose Bowl Wolverines fans didn't feel the same electric assuredness as the previous game in Ann Arbor. In fact, it felt like Washington State came out to start the game looking like the better team. It wasn't until Woodson's interception of WSU quarterback Ryan Leaf in the end zone in the second quarter that the Wolverines started to feel more like the team we'd become accustomed to seeing. That pick not only saved Michigan from going down two touchdowns, but it provided the spark that they needed to start playing Wolverine football.

Woodson may have been the spark in that game, but it was Griese who kept the fire going. He completed 18 of 30 passes on the day for 251 yards and three touchdown passes and led Michigan football someplace it hadn't been in forty-nine years. The 21–16 win over the Cougars capped off a season that had begun with Coach Carr handing out pick axes as a visual metaphor at the beginning of fall camp. The message was that no person attempting to climb a mountain reaches the top alone. No man is more important than the team … the team, the team, the team. The Michigan Wolverines were back at the summit of college football.

Wolverines coach Lloyd Carr enjoys a moment after the 1998 Rose Bowl win with linebacker Rob Swett. The Wolverines were named 1997 national champions after that game by the Associated Press. *Photo by Sara Stillman. Courtesy of Bentley Historical Library, University of Michigan.*

## Charles Woodson, 1997 Heisman Trophy Winner

Michigan had just won the game that would secure its first national championship since 1948, and the euphoric Wolverines gathered on a small stage that had been assembled at midfield immediately after their Rose Bowl victory over Washington State.

Charles Woodson was in the middle of the unabashed joy, and rightfully so. The Heisman Trophy-winning cornerback had turned the tide early in the game with blitzes and a key interception, and he handed momentum over to quarterback Brian Griese, who knew just what to do with it en route to a 21–16 triumph.

Woodson, nodding his head and smiling, looked at Griese and said, "We did it, baby! We did it! National champions! They can't say nothing now."

Griese nodded and rubbed Woodson's head, while co-captain Jon Jansen put his huge right arm around Woodson and slapped his right shoulder. Coach Lloyd Carr turned back to gently pat Woodson's cheek. Teammates shrieked and whooped for joy as the Rose Bowl trophy was brought before them.

That was what it felt like to win the 12th and final game in an undefeated season.

"After we won the Rose Bowl," said Woodson, "the next twenty-four hours were like a blur. But I think about being up on the podium after the game, and that's the one thing that sticks out in my mind because it was the end of a chapter.

"It closed the book on a very special season in which we worked harder than ever to reach that podium. So everybody wants to win a championship, but who puts in the work and sacrifice to do it gets it. And for us to be up on that podium after the game and to know that we were national champions, we knew that what we put into it made all the difference.

"It was one of the best moments in my life to be able to say, 'I'm a national champion.'"

It takes a team to win a national championship, but it takes special players to step up when it matters most.

That was Woodson—the ultimate gamer.

He was defined by not only his versatility, but by coming up clutch in big games. And there was none bigger than the final game he played as a Wolverine.

Woodson's interception early in the second quarter was perhaps the biggest play of the game.

Washington State was knocking on the door at the Michigan 12 yard line and was one play away from taking a two-touchdown lead. Quarterback Ryan Leaf rolled to his left, making for an awkward throwing release for the big right-hander. He let loose a wobbly pass that Woodson jumped in front of receiver Kevin McKenzie to pick off.

Woodson rolled to the turf in the end zone, regained his footing by doing a somersault, and was mobbed by teammates. A fan in the stands held up a sign: "CHARLES IN CHARGE."

Griese threw a touchdown pass to Tai Streets later in the quarter to tie the score, and Michigan had averted the need for a long comeback attempt.

Charles Woodson, the 1997 Heisman Trophy winner, cele-
brates in the second quarter of Michigan's Rose Bowl win
over Washington State on January 1, 1998.
*AP Photo/Mark J. Terrill.*

Woodson assured that the Wolverines reached the game that meant everything
in Pasadena by doing just about everything possible to beat Ohio State in the regular season finale in Ann Arbor.

He took a punt return 78 yards, getting superb blocking, breaking the one
tackle he had to, and racing to six points. Woodson intended to duplicate the
Heisman Trophy pose Desmond Howard did in that same south end zone at Michigan Stadium, but teammates piled atop him before he could get in position.

Woodson wasn't done, though.

He caught a 37-yard pass from Griese to set up another touchdown.

He intercepted Buckeye quarterback Stanley Jackson to thwart a Buckeye
comeback attempt.

Michigan radio play-by-play announcer Frank Beckmann proclaimed: "Polish off the Heisman! Make room on the mantel! Charles Woodson took it away—an end zone interception!"

And when it was all over, the Wolverines had a 20–14 win, and Woodson earned the right to have the final say with OSU receiver David Boston, who had predicted big things for himself and the Buckeyes that day, and even physically got into it with Woodson on one play.

Woodson proclaimed: "They do all the talkin', I do the walkin', baby." Then he walked off the field with a long-stemmed red rose clenched in his teeth.

"That was one of those iconic moments," Woodson said during the team's twentieth-anniversary celebration at Crisler Center. "It's one of those moments that when you see it now, you associate it with that game.

"My first two years, we played Ohio State as spoilers [and won]. Now, it was our turn. We were on top, and they were coming in and trying to play spoilers. So we had to come out and really bite down. We knew just what they were thinking. In '95, they were undefeated coming in, and we beat them. We didn't want to let that thing happen to us.

"And so, when the '97 game was over, I put the rose in my mouth and that was the exclamation mark. We knew what went into that game and working hard and doing it right. We told them so. So putting that rose in my mouth was a statement."

Woodson, with "The Victors" playing loudly in the background at the Crisler reunion, was told they were playing his song.

"You bet!" he said with a smile.

He then answered one last question about Lloyd Carr's impact on him.

"Lloyd was a tough coach," said Woodson. "He was a hard coach, and so he made you focus. So, I felt that, for us, because of his tough coaching he brought the best or the worst out of you. But, for that particular season, the strings he pulled on each player is what turned us into champions.

"I appreciate Lloyd, man. He's a tough coach, but he was a great guy and human being. So he had a great positive impact on me and all of us."

Carr would visit his players in their hotel rooms the night before each game, and he ended the brief talks by wishing them good luck the next day.

Woodson told Carr one night, "Coach, I don't need any luck."

Carr ended that story by smiling and adding, "And, he didn't."

Woodson was so good that even when Michigan State quarterback Todd Schultz once attempted to throw the ball away as defensive end Juaquin Feazell closed on him near the sideline, Woodson picked it off.

That interception in East Lansing in 1997 was the most spectacular play in three seasons of spectacular plays for Woodson. He rose so high that ABC-TV analyst Bill Curry said Schultz "has no idea that Charles Woodson can jump fifteen feet in the air" before snatching the ball with his right hand, cradling it into his body while falling to the ground, and dragging his left foot in bounds.

Jim Brandstatter, the longtime radio voice of Michigan football, noted: "Charles Woodson had big games in big games. Woodson just stood up, and the moment was never too big for Charles."

Woodson had eight interceptions and nine pass breakups along with 44 tackles as a junior in 1997, finishing second on Michigan's career interception list with 18.

Carr asked him to provide spot play at tailback after his freshman season—Woodson ran for 2,028 yards as a senior at Fremont (Ohio) Ross—because Tshimanga Biakabutuka had just left for the NFL after his junior season, but Woodson declined. But he said he would play receiver when needed and Carr integrated him into the offense.

Woodson had 36 offensive touches in his sophomore and junior seasons that produced 575 yards (16.0 yards per touch) with five touchdowns. He had 25 catches, 11 runs mostly on reverses, and two pass completions.

"You'd better know where he was in the game," said Carr, who enjoyed keeping defensive coordinators off balance with Woodson. "He had explosive speed. Charles just had a burst."

The offense gave him added notoriety, but Woodson became the only primarily defensive player to ever win the Heisman. He had 433 first-place votes and 1,815 points compared to the 281 first-place votes and 1,543 points of Tennessee quarterback Peyton Manning, who finished second and ironically visited Michigan as a high school recruit.

Woodson also was a two-time All-American and three-time All-Big Ten first team selection who claimed the Walter Camp Award, Bronko Nagurski Trophy, Chuck Bednarik Award, and Jim Thorpe Award. He became the 31st Wolverine inducted into the College Football Hall of Fame in 2018.

The nine-time Pro Bowl selection is a shoo-in for the Pro Football Hall of Fame. Woodson made 65 interceptions, 1,003 tackles, 28 forced fumbles, and 20 sacks in 18 seasons with the Oakland Raiders and Green Bay Packers, with whom he won a Super Bowl.

Part Four

Upon his retirement after the 2015 season, at age thirty-nine, Woodson became part of ESPN's *Sunday NFL Countdown* and *Monday Night Countdown* broadcast teams, proprietor of Charles Woodson Wines in the Napa Valley, and he focused more time and money on the charities he supports.

Woodson was invited back to Michigan Stadium as an honorary captain for the 2017 Ohio State game. He attended with his wife, April, and sons, Charles Jr. and Chase, and when introduced on the field the fans gave him a rousing standing ovation.

Celebrating with Charles Woodson never gets old.

# Brian Griese's Emotional Journey with His Father and Their Pasadena Hug

Brian Griese saved what was arguably his best college performance for his final game as a Wolverine.

Griese passed for 251 yards with three touchdowns and one interception in Michigan's 21–16 Rose Bowl win over Washington State on January 1, 1998.

The late Keith Jackson, perhaps the best play-by-play announcer college football has ever had, announced in his folksy manner as the Wolverines celebrated the victory and undefeated season on the field: "The MVP—I'm standing beside his proud Daddy … Go ahead and cry."

Bob Griese, the color analyst for that game on ABC-TV, had his eyes well up with tears.

"I've done well all year," said the father, who usually insisted on calling his youngest son "Griese" while describing the Wolverine quarterback on broadcasts. "but, well, this is special."

Brian said he was taken aback by that scene when finally able to view it, noting that his father is loving but seldom emotional.

"I've got a question!" Jackson demanded on air. "Did his old man ever win this trophy?"

His father also led his team, Purdue, to victory over USC in Pasadena by a 14–13 score on January 2, 1967. But that was a defensive struggle, and both Boilermaker touchdowns came on short runs with Griese adding the point-after kicks. The MVP of that game was Purdue defensive back John Charles.

Now, the father had plenty of accomplishments. He was elected to both the College Football Hall of Fame and Pro Football Hall of Fame, leading the Miami

Dolphins to two Super Bowl wins and his own perfect season in 1972. But his son had the Rose Bowl MVP on him.

"After the game," said Brian, "I saw my dad in the hallway underneath the stadium going to talk to you guys in the media room. We didn't say a word. We just hugged each other, and it was a special moment. That was the moment that—we'd been through a lot, losing my mom—it's still there. It's right under the skin."

His mother, Judi, died of breast cancer in 1988, and the two older Griese boys were on their own. Brian and Bob became closer than ever. They were everything to each other. Bob had remarried to Shay, and life went on. But they couldn't help but think of losing Judi in their joy. She had been gone nearly thirty years when we spoke with Brian about that Pasadena moment twenty years ago. And he once again became very emotional, fighting back tears. That hug with his father always will tug at his heartstrings.

Brian wasn't even supposed to be the best quarterback in that Rose Bowl. That was Washington State's Ryan Leaf, who became the No. 2 overall pick in the upcoming NFL draft, while Griese went in the third round to the Denver Broncos. But Brian was the star of stars that afternoon.

Griese's last game in Michigan Stadium was a memorable victory over Ohio State that earned the Big Ten title and sent the Wolverines to Pasadena. He got carried off the field on the shoulders of his teammates while holding a long-stemmed red rose.

His father and Jackson also broadcast that game and surprised him hours later.

"I had a party at my house," said Griese. "It was kind of an impromptu thing, and a bunch of the guys came over. The funny memory that I have is [Glen] Steele and [Zach] Adami and everybody's in my little house we were renting in that neighborhood over by the Blue Front. And the door opens, and we didn't know who was coming in. And in walks … Keith Jackson."

Griese dragged out the pronunciation of the legendary announcer's first and last names and paused.

"And then my dad walks in behind him," Griese continued. "And the whole room stops and looks up, and they both say, 'Congratulations!' We had a great time, and celebrating with my dad and Keith after that was pretty cool.

"It was fun; it was a good memory."

Griese was 3–0 against the Buckeyes, with two wins coming in starts and the 1996 victory coming in relief.

For all Griese did in Michigan's 1997 national championship season, there was nothing more pivotal than his ability to right the ship in the second half on October

18 in Ann Arbor. The Wolverines had fallen behind Iowa, 21–7, and Griese had thrown three interceptions. Two of them led to Hawkeye touchdowns.

How Griese handled himself in the halftime locker room set the tone for a comeback.

"Guys, that's the worst half of football I've ever played," Griese said. "I'm going to go out there and play the best half."

Offensive tackle Jon Jansen said, "There was no, 'woe is me' in him. We all felt the confidence."

Griese engineered a 71-yard drive on the first possession of the second half, finishing it with a 10-yard touchdown pass to Russell Shaw.

Two drives later, Griese ran the final yard on a 67-yard drive for the touchdown to make it 21-all.

Griese's 2-yard touchdown pass to All-America tight end Jerame Tuman capped a 77-yard drive with 2:55 remaining to play for Michigan's first lead of the game.

Final score: Michigan 28, Iowa 24.

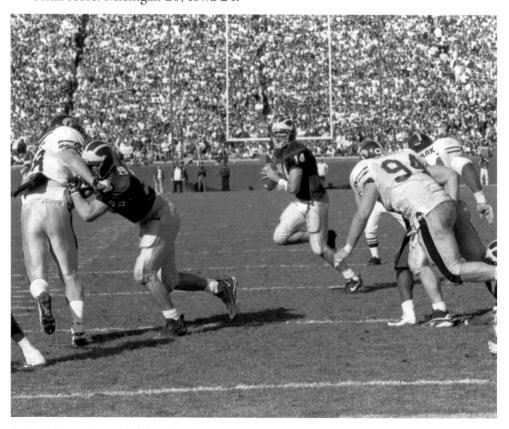

Brian Griese rolls to his right to throw the game-winning touchdown pass to tight end Jerame Tuman in the pivotal, comeback win over Iowa in the undefeated 1997 season that ended with a national championship.
*Photo by Robert Kalmbach.*
*Courtesy of Bentley Historical Library, University of Michigan.*

Still, Griese had to turn around his career before he could be trusted to turn around games. He was a holder on placement kicks as a freshman, started 10 games as an injury replacement during his sophomore and junior seasons, and did not become the established starter until he was a fifth-year senior.

He also was arrested for a minor incident at the Scorekeepers sports bar in Ann Arbor and tried Coach Lloyd Carr's patience in other ways, too. But Brian took the punishment, learned from his mistakes, and became a shining example of grabbing opportunity before it gets away.

Carr recalled what he saw happen in 1997: "All spring and summer he was working as hard as he could. He got in the best shape of his life; he matured, he grew up. He was everything you wanted."

Griese threw for 2,293 yards with 17 touchdowns and only six interceptions in 1997 and was named first team All-Big Ten.

Receiver Tai Streets, who hooked up with Griese on two touchdown passes in the Rose Bowl, said, "Griese was just outstanding all year."

Griese was the recruiting host to Jansen, a co-captain in 1997, and he watched him persevere and grow from walk-on to All-Conference.

"Brian's career at Michigan was always overshadowed by these big recruits coming in," said Jansen. "Scott Dreisbach came in and started as a redshirt freshman [in 1995] and then you've got Tom Brady [one year behind Dreisbach]. And there was Jason Kapsner coming in from Minnesota who was supposed to be the next great thing. So there were all these quarterbacks everyone was talking about, including Scot Loeffler, who came in with Brian. Loeffler had a shoulder injury and never really had a chance to play.

"And Brian just always showed up and did his work, and had one incident. But for four years opportunity didn't present itself. In the fifth year, they have this battle, and they gave him the ball and said, 'This team is yours. Let's go!' And he was ready."

What enabled Griese to make it through all the challenges?

"He was never too high, never too low," said Jansen. "He could seem aloof. And sometimes people would say, 'I'm not sure he cares about it.' But that wasn't true. In my opinion, what you need is a guy who gets in the huddle, and is in control no matter what the situation is. When Brian runs forty yards against Penn State, and the only thing he's trying to do is catch his breath to call the next play. He's not cheering. It's what's next, and I think that's really what served him so well during all of those four years when he didn't play. It was always: 'What's next?'"

Griese had other major college scholarship offers but chose to walk on initially at Michigan, which had built a reputation for producing NFL quarterbacks. He left No. 5 in school career passing yardage with 4,383, ranking behind only Elvis Grbac, Todd Collins, Jim Harbaugh, and Steve Smith at the time.

Griese won a Super Bowl with Denver while backing up John Elway, was selected to the 2000 Pro Bowl team, and threw for 19,440 yards in 11 NFL seasons.

He did even bigger things off the field.

Griese, in 2015, won the Big Ten's Ford-Kinnick Leadership Award, named for 1934 Michigan MVP and 38th President of the US Gerald Ford and 1940 Heisman Trophy winner Nile Kinnick. Griese also won the conference's Dungy-Thompson Humanitarian Award in 2014 and became the first Big Ten player to ever win both of those awards.

Brian founded Judi's House in 2002, named in honor of his mother, with a mission to help grieving children and their caregivers in the Denver area, and the organization expanded its reach by developing a curriculum shared around the country.

He also helped establish the Champions for Children's Hearts golf weekend in 2007 along with 1997 championship teammates Steve Hutchinson and Charles Woodson. The event helped fund construction and the development of a congenital heart center at Michigan's Mott Children's Hospital.

Brian became a college football analyst for ESPN in 2009 and hooked up with his father to write a book, *Undefeated*, which chronicled their lives during perfect football seasons and living through and leaning upon one another after losing Judi to cancer.

Their emotional hug after Michigan's win in Pasadena said even more about life's triumphs than football's victories.

## Tom Brady: Learning to Believe in Himself

Tom Brady had to climb the ladder, and it was a definite struggle getting up those rungs. He huffed and puffed and pulled upward with all of his might. But he was having difficulty getting anywhere near that top rung and sometimes seemed to be reaching in vain.

He started out fifth on the quarterback depth chart at Michigan, and Brady became frustrated that his dreams weren't coming true.

So he took the advice of a teammate and visited Greg Harden, a counselor in the athletic department who several years earlier had done so much for Desmond Howard's mental approach while he sought to break into the starting lineup.

"My favorite people are self-referrals," said Harden. "It's the kid who knocks on your door and says, 'I need your help. I heard you could help.' So Tom [Brady] shows up and says, 'I'm struggling, and I refuse to fall apart. And I want to talk to you. I want to be the starting quarterback at Michigan.'"

Harden responded: "Son, there's nothing I can do about that. But I can get you to believe, if no one else believes, that you're the man to do it."

Brady nodded and said, "Let's start there."

He was recovering from acute appendicitis, had lost twenty pounds, and dropped out of serious contention for the job he coveted.

"He was borderline depressed and as skinny as a rail," Harden recalled. "He's a tad bit distraught, and we began to talk about how important it was for him to believe in himself even though nobody else was.

"Our whole mission was: 'Tom, all that matters is what you think!' That's all we talked about. And Tom [eventually] got into the starting lineup, but he was anxious and nervous, looking to the sideline, worried about being pulled. I said, 'Son, when are you going to accept that you're the starting quarterback? Stop it! You've got to believe. Make mistakes and make them with enthusiasm—just don't repeat them.'"

Harden watched closely at games to make sure Brady was broken of the habit of looking toward coaches when he erred. They kept meeting every Friday before games, and the pupil continued improving, week after week.

The mentor was ecstatic about what Brady had become and recalled his greatest moment at Michigan, which came in his final college game.

"His Orange Bowl performance was a signature game," said Harden, "and it's the game you see him playing over and over again in the NFL, where he's just not going to lose. And those cats believed in him, they trusted him, and that was because he had total confidence in himself. When he finishes here, he is clear about who he is, where he is going, and what it will take for him to get there."

Brady led the Wolverines to a 35–34 overtime win over Alabama, throwing for 369 yards and four touchdowns with zero interceptions in the Orange Bowl, and he never looked back. When he first met New England Patriots owner Robert Kraft, Brady looked him in the eyes and said, 'I'm the best decision this organization has ever made.'"

He believed that deeply in himself despite being a sixth-round pick.

The 199th player selected back in 2000 won five Super Bowls, more than any quarterback in history, before turning forty, and many consider him the greatest to ever play the position in the NFL. It all began with a belief in himself that has conquered all—including a 28–3 deficit against the Atlanta Falcons in the Super Bowl on February 5, 2017. Brady threw for a Super Bowl–record 466 yards to spearhead a stunning comeback for a 34–28 win.

Incidentally, Howard (Super Bowl MVP in 1997 game for the Green Bay Packers) and Brady (four Super Bowl MVP selections) combine to give Michigan five Super Bowl MVPs, equaling the total of the other thirteen schools in the Big Ten combined.

Brady and Howard, whom Harden called "the two most coachable cats I'd ever met," are among the many Wolverines who heard the question from Harden that is at the core of his approach:

"What kind of person do you want to be?"

Examining that question, says Harden, is what allows them to establish self-worth that can't be measured in touchdowns, baskets, goals or speed.

"Imagine telling Tom Brady and Desmond Howard that they've got to decide, with or without football, that life is going to be amazing," said Harden. "What I am suggesting at that moment is that you have got to decide that your life is worth it whether football works or not.

"Then, football no longer becomes the idol god. Instead of being a football player, you become a man who happens to play football, and you just happen to play it better than most. My whole mission is to convince somebody that they are a whole person and that football is a vehicle that they are to use for self-expression. But their self-worth and self-esteem must not be based on performance."

He calls Brady and Howard "the poster boys" for his work.

Brady recalled his difficult, up-the-ladder climb as a Wolverine prior to the 2013 season, when he addressed the Michigan players in the main team meeting room that is set up just like a large movie theater, with its rows of cushioned seats angled upward from the floor where Brady spoke.

"I didn't have an easy experience," Brady began. "I didn't come in as a top-rated recruit, I didn't come in with an opportunity to play right away, I had to earn it.

"And do you know what the greatest honor I've ever received as a player is? In my fourth year and my fifth year, I was named team captain. That, to this day, is the single greatest achievement I've ever had as a football player.

"Because the men in this room chose me to lead their team. And these were my best friends. These were the guys that knew that I liked to work. That knew that I loved football. That knew that I loved to play. They knew that I wanted to be the quarterback for Michigan."

Brady discussed how important the Michigan program remained to him, his former teammates and to those who came before him. He stressed how each player currently in the Michigan program had a responsibility to everyone else who has "ever worn this helmet."

He told the seniors to cherish their final moments on campus. He told the freshmen to be patient and the underclassmen to seize any opportunity they had in front of them.

And, in conclusion, he quoted Bo Schembechler's mantra.

"Those who stay will be champions," Brady said. "What does that mean to you? It means you stick around, you fight, you work, and you do everything you can for each other.

"And you'll be a champion."

Three years later, in Jim Harbaugh's second season as the head coach at their alma mater, Brady returned as an honorary captain for a game and took the field with the current captains for the coin toss. He also talked to the team once again.

"It was basically a chilling speech," defensive tackle Ryan Glasgow said. "It made the hair on the back of your neck stand up."

Quarterback Wilton Speight added, "It made me realize maybe the greatest quarterback of all time was saying that I represent him. That got me in the mindset that I wanted to go out and play even better than he ever did."

Harbaugh was asked that day if he felt Brady could one day be his quarterbacks coach. He noted, "That would be phenomenal" before jokingly stating, "Head coach here someday. Quarterback coach, coordinator, head coach."

When asked if he would actually step aside for Brady, Harbaugh laughed and added, "For Tom Brady, I will give him a deep, long bow, shake hands, and I'll coach the quarterbacks for him."

It was a pretty cool day. The best quarterback Michigan has ever had as a collegiate player—Harbaugh, who finished third in 1986 Heisman Trophy voting—and the best quarterback any college has ever had in the NFL got to meet, talk, and even play catch prior to the game with Colorado.

"When I look back on my career of playing catch with people, that was right up there with my dad," Harbaugh said. "Tom has a good arm. He throws such a good ball. That ball almost catches itself. I wish I wouldn't have given him the wind."

Brady, who began his NFL career as an unheralded backup to Drew Bledsoe, learned how to work his way to the top at Michigan.

There are those who thought, after Brady dropped down that depth chart in his early seasons, that he might have been better off signing with baseball's Montreal Expos, who drafted the power-hitting catcher from San Mateo (California) Junipero Serra High School in the 18th round in 1995. Baseball scouts believed he would have been drafted much higher had it not been for his football scholarship, and they loved his arm and intangibles.

Serra, an all-boys Catholic school located south of San Francisco, is a sports powerhouse. It has produced Barry Bonds, Jim Fregosi, and Gregg Jefferies in baseball and Lynn Swann in football.

However, the Expos never got into serious negotiations with Brady because he and his parents, Galynn and Tom Sr., had decided they wanted him to go to college.

Brady, though, was not a prep All-America. He was a solid prospect with a strong arm, good touch on his passes, and a great head on his shoulders. So he was recruited to fill the bill as the quarterback the Wolverines include in each and every class.

He had definite potential, but there were plenty of players in front of him when he was a freshman in 1995: Scott Dreisbach, Brian Griese, Jason Carr, and Scot Loeffler. Griese and Dreisbach would start in the NFL, but none had the sort of universal acclaim coming out of high school to scare off Brady. Peyton Manning might very well have sent Brady in another direction with another school, though. Manning made an official visit to Ann Arbor and would have been behind senior Todd Collins as a freshman in 1994 had he selected the Wolverines.

There was also a great player coming in behind Brady—one who received attention that rivaled Manning's coming out of high school. Drew Henson was considered perhaps the finest quarterback the state of Michigan had ever produced, and the Brighton High three-sport star committed to Coach Lloyd Carr after his junior season of 1996.

Henson also was a baseball superstar. The New York Yankees drafted him in the third round, and he played in the minor leagues for them during summers while attending college. That provided Brady an edge in getting to better know his teammates and particularly his receivers in the offseason. He held off the young phenom, and it became his team.

Brady mostly carried a clipboard during the 1997 national championship season, when he played behind Griese. But once he got the reins, Brady went 20–5 as a starter and led the team to a co-Big Ten championship in 1998 and that Orange Bowl win over Alabama in his last game as a Wolverine.

Brady put up solid numbers in his final two seasons, passing for 5,351 yards and 35 touchdowns, but the best honor he could manage was honorable mention All-Conference in 1999. If you are looking for a quality sports trivia question, ask for the name of the Big Ten's first-team quarterback selected ahead of both Brady and Drew Brees in 1999. The All-Big Ten first-team quarterback on teams voted upon by both the coaches and the media that year was Ohio State's Joe Germaine. The second-team choice was Purdue's Brees, who also became an NFL superstar with the New Orleans Saints.

Quarterback Tom Brady readies for the snap from center David Brandt with offensive guard Steve Hutchinson to the far right and tailback Anthony Thomas behind him.
*Photo by Robert Kalmbach.*
*Courtesy of Bentley Historical Library, University of Michigan.*

Brady had succeeded. After knocking on Harden's door and proclaiming that he wanted to be the starting quarterback, he learned to believe in himself, and in turn his coaches and teammates believed in him.

That belief became the foundation for everything Thomas Edward Patrick Brady Jr. accomplished for the Wolverines and then the Patriots. It set his greatness in motion.

## Braylon Edwards, Record-Breaking Receiver

Braylon Edwards became the most prolific pass-catcher in the history of Michigan football, making more catches for more yards and scoring more touchdowns than anyone who came before him.

And, make no mistake about it, that bar was set plenty high for Braylon when he arrived in 2001.

The Wolverines previously had a pair of three-time All-Americas who were among the best players in the history of college football. There was Bennie Oosterbaan in the middle of the Roaring Twenties, and Anthony Carter in the early 1980s.

It was the school and conference records of Carter, the elusive A.C. who played with Braylon's father at Michigan, who inspired Edwards to greatness.

Then there was Desmond Howard, the 1991 Heisman Trophy winner, and one of only two players who were exclusively receivers to win that award.

So if you want to get remembered as a receiver at Michigan, you better not only rewrite the record books. You had best dominate games as well.

Edwards did both.

His heroic performance down the stretch against Michigan State in Ann Arbor on October 30, 2004, is one of the most electrifying the program's fans have ever witnessed.

The Wolverines trailed Michigan State by 17 points with 8:43 remaining in the fourth quarter, but Edwards went up and caught two touchdowns in the right corner of the end zone from quarterback Chad Henne to force overtime and then the game-winning, 24-yard scoring pass on a slant route on a 3rd-and-nine play in the third overtime of a raucous 45–37 comeback victory.

"It's crazy," said Edwards, who had 11 catches for 189 yards and a 22-yard run on a reverse play in that game. "When it happened, I was only twenty-one, and you never know how you are impacting longtime fans and kids. Now, [all these] years later, I still have kids coming up to me saying that game made their life or that I was their idol.

"And then there are older adults. Yeah, I was No. 1, but A.C. will forever be No. 1 to them. That's their guy from their era. But in that game, the older fans were like, 'A.C.'s my guy, but what you did was special.' That was the seal-of-approval game."

Braylon Edwards, Michigan's record-setting receiver, runs past Michigan State cornerback As-
ton Watson (No. 12) on his touchdown catch in the third overtime to beat Michigan State, 45–37,
in a comeback win on October 30, 2004.
*AP Photo/Carlos Osorio.*

It was his signature game, but what he put his mind to accomplishing a dozen
years later provided his signature move as a student-athlete.

And when Edwards decided to finish his degree at Michigan, a friend sent him a video of *Back to School*, a 1986 movie starring Rodney Dangerfield about a man attending college with his son.

"I busted out laughing," Edwards said. "That perfect dive of his [into a swimming pool] at the end of that movie can't be beat."

Edwards, then thirty-four, ended up getting the last laugh, though, on a bright, sunny Saturday in April 2017, when he walked across the stage to pick up his college diploma at Michigan Stadium, the scene of his athletic triumphs as well.

"Now my parents can wave and scream and cry and cheer," said Edwards, whose parents are Malesa Plater and former Wolverines and NFL running back Stanley Edwards.

Braylon's general studies degree focused on marketing strategies.

"I think that should be the first dream of any student—to make sure you walk across that stage," said Edwards. "Education is the thing that's going to be there for the long haul. Sports is fine, but it's a long shot to play for a long time.

"Now, I didn't wrap my mind around this concept for a long time. But even if you play a while, you retire as a relatively young man in the eyes of the world. A degree is something that can never be taken from you, and a degree from the University of Michigan is powerful on so many levels."

He left school a dozen years prior without the diploma but did drive out of town in style.

Edwards had a Bentley coupe delivered the day before his workout for pro scouts in 2005. He drove it a bit, parked it in a garage at his condo, and opted to drive his Ford Explorer to pro day.

"The Bentley wasn't the message I wanted to send," said Edwards. "So I pull up in the Explorer and Lloyd's there. He says to me, 'Where's that Bentley at?' I asked Lloyd, 'So you saw me drive that?' He said, 'Saw you? I heard it. I want to go for a ride.' A couple days later, Lloyd and I met at Schembechler Hall, and I took him for a ride.

"And how about this: I almost ran out of gas because when they dropped it off, I didn't think to put gas in it. So I almost ran out of gas, and Lloyd said, 'Damn it! Same old Braylon.' So we ended up getting some lunch, and I took him back to Schembechler, but that was cool."

Did Carr spring for some gas money?

"Nah," Edwards said with a chuckle, "but I did tell Lloyd, 'Now you can legally give me some money.'"

Edwards had plenty of that after the Cleveland Browns made him the third overall pick in the first round of the 2005 draft.

Edwards had one monster season in the NFL, making the Pro Bowl after catching 80 passes for 1,289 yards and 16 touchdowns for the Browns in 2007. He played eight years, making 359 catches for 5,522 yards and 40 touchdowns, but was done after spending 2012 with the Seattle Seahawks and New York Jets.

"I finally had some downtime and wasn't working for a network or radio station per se," said Edwards. "So it was time for me to assess what the future held for me. I had a meeting with a good buddy of mine, the athletic director, Warde Manuel.

"We sat down, and I congratulated him on coming back to Michigan. Then we talked about myself. We talked about stripping away Braylon Edwards the football player and creating Braylon Edwards the second phase. He suggested finishing my degree was the number one thing I needed to do."

And so No. 1 on the Wolverines football roster, 2001-2004, accepted that "No. 1" challenge of Manuel.

"When Warde makes a suggestion," said Edwards, "it's really more than a suggestion. It's what you need to do. So I took him at his word and enrolled."

The numeral Edwards wore has been special at Michigan ever since Carter made it so. Braylon added to the lore of that number and then some. He still holds Michigan's career record for catches (252), yards (3,541), and touchdowns (39), exceeding Carter's touchdown total by two while also establishing a new Big Ten record.

Braylon said that record means the most to him because it takes into account every receiver who ever played in the conference.

"Growing up," said Edwards, "that's all my dad talked about was A.C.'s footwork or A.C.'s ability to catch the ball in traffic or A.C.'s route running or how he returned punts. A.C. was the best. Growing up, I said, 'I'm tired of hearing about A.C.' But not in a bad way. I knew I wanted to go to Michigan, play wide out, and wear No. 1. I wanted to beat all his records and everything he did. So that was my motivation since middle school.

"When I got to Michigan and had a down day or a bad practice, I remembered why I was there. So having No. 1 has been special to me my whole life. Following in the footsteps of my dad and A.C.—it's now thirty-five years after they played—meant so much."

Edwards won the Biletnikoff Award as the nation's top wide receiver in 2004 and set school single-season receiving records with 97 catches for 1,330 yards. His

15 touchdown receptions that season are second only to the 19 Howard caught in 1991.

Some of the students he attended classes with upon going "back to school" were preschoolers when he last played for the Wolverines, and nearly all of them were under ten years old. Yet several recognized him and wanted to talk football.

"I walked through the door in this class, and you could see the excitement on this guy's face," said Edwards. "He was just ready to talk to me, but he waited for an opportunity. We got on an elevator together, and he said, 'I've got to tell you, Michigan-Michigan State, in '04, oh my God!' The guy played lacrosse, and that was pretty neat."

Edwards continued doing analyst work for FOX Sports, the Big Ten Network, and CBS Radio, but added that he was prepared for future business ventures and can finally be more than a silent investor in projects.

"I can come up with my own marketing strategy as it relates to dealing with marketing and branding for a firm," said Edwards, who lives in West Bloomfield, Michigan. "I'll have more channels open to me."

Edwards was twenty credit hours away from his degree when he went to the NFL, and he got those credits in the 2016–17 school year.

Edwards, in the days leading up to graduation, tweeted @OfficialBraylon a photo of his cap and gown and this message: "One week from today #Blessed."

That said it all.

"I didn't have to worry about football when I came back to school," said Edwards. "I was really able to pay attention to the other kids in class, the presentations, the professors, and anybody on campus.

"Michigan's a special place. They don't call us 'the leaders and best' for no reason. The professors are the best of the best, energetic and enthusiastic and smart. They have wisdom on top of wisdom, and the kids are the smartest of the smart. It was the first time I really paid that side full attention, and I was proud to be getting a degree from Michigan.

"Now, I wouldn't be having classes with these geniuses if there wasn't something about me that stood out. That's what I paid attention to this second time around as just a student."

Dangerfield, playing Thornton Melon in *Back to School*, was a millionaire who discovered he couldn't buy an education.

Edwards returned to school after a lucrative pro football career and discovered exactly what makes an education truly special.

Braylon Jamel Edwards got it all—the records, the fame, and the degree.

# Coach Jim Harbaugh

Wolverines fans had the stars align perfectly when Jim Harbaugh was named head coach on December 30, 2014.

Harbaugh, Michigan's All-America quarterback twenty-eight years prior, went on to a standout NFL career before becoming the head coach at the University of San Diego and Stanford. He won big at both schools and moved on to the San Francisco 49ers, which he took to the Super Bowl and three NFC championship games in four seasons.

But just how could a star NFL coach return to college, even his own alma mater?

Two factors played into making it happen, and the first one was timing. Harbaugh and the people he worked for in San Francisco weren't on the same page, and they parted ways by mutual agreement. The Wolverines finished a disappointing season with a 5–7 record, and coach Brady Hoke was fired.

Still, Harbaugh would've had his pick of virtually any NFL opening at that time. Something else had come into play for serendipity to occur.

And that all-important element was just how deeply Harbaugh cared for and loved Michigan.

I was fortunate enough to be at a breakfast at the Jack Roth Stadium Club in Michigan Stadium before Harbaugh was announced as the coach of the Wolverines. We got reacquainted before the press conference downstairs.

Jim sat there on padded chairs with five of his children, munching cereal and bananas and soaking in the view of Michigan Stadium, a place where their father played and their grandfather, Jack, coached.

Harbaugh picked up Jack, two, wearing a knit cap with a block M on it and hugged him as he looked at the field below. He soaked up the moment, thinking back to past glories and ahead to the future.

The warm glow of that moment told you why he had left the NFL.

Harbaugh had come home.

I asked him that morning about the timing of his hiring, and when becoming the Michigan coach began going through his mind.

"I can honestly say it's gone through my mind since I was a youngster of nine or ten," said Harbaugh, whom coach Bo Schembechler once caught as a young boy sitting in his chair, feet up on his desk, at his office in Weidenbach Hall.

"I dreamed about being the coach at Michigan, and now it's time to live that dream. It's a dream I've had since I was little … I didn't really take a pros-and-cons approach. I just went with my heart. I never had a list. I kept coming back to coming back here."

Jim wanted his youngest children—Addison, Katherine, and Jack—to attend St. Francis of Assisi School and drive their bikes to practices after classes, just as he and his siblings had. He wanted them to have the best years of their lives exactly where he did.

The Harbaugh mantra—"Who has it better than us?"—came from his father, who would quote it during family times.

Jack and Jackie, his parents, moved in right down the block from them on the same secluded street on the east side of town where, ironically, Schembechler once lived. And Jack, who was a head coach at Western Michigan and Western Kentucky, became an advisor to his son at Michigan. Jay Harbaugh, the Wolverines' running backs coach and special teams assistant, is on his father's staff.

So family ties were at the root of Jim returning to Michigan.

And the stars came out when Harbaugh came home.

He initiated a "Signing of the Stars" show on campus to celebrate signing day for recruits, and both former Michigan quarterback Tom Brady and Wolverines baseball signee Derek Jeter (who went straight to the pros and never played at Michigan) turned out for the first one in February of 2015.

"First and foremost, Jim's brought a lot of excitement back to the program," said Jeter, who retired in 2014 after cementing his first-ballot Hall of Fame status as the shortstop and captain of the New York Yankees. "He's got people talking about Michigan, which is good.

"He's got not just members of the media but fans and everybody talking about Michigan. He makes it fun; he makes it exciting. As a fan, looking at it, this is how it should be."

Brady had a lengthy conversation with Harbaugh about returning to Michigan before he took the job and helped recruit him back home.

"Jim's the perfect fit," said Brady. "But it was a lot of people above me who brought him back. It's great to have a great leader like that.

"I think anyone who has played here loves the school, loves the tradition. It's just the place to be."

Harbaugh had Brady serve as an honorary captain for a game, and he joked that someday he would be willing to step aside to coach on Brady's Michigan staff.

Jim's former teammates and those who have played for the Wolverines were thrilled with his return and watched his first three seasons with much interest.

Jim Harbaugh (left) and Rick Leach inside Harbaugh's office at Schembechler Hall. Both were All-American quarterbacks for Bo Schembechler, with a combined seven seasons as Michigan's starter. A photo from the 1987 Rose Bowl that Schembechler autographed to Harbaugh is on the wall behind them.
*Photo Courtesy of Rick Leach.*

Rick Leach, the quarterback Harbaugh idolized when his father coached Michigan's defensive backs, said, "I know there was a push with former players and special Michigan people involved in it. Jimmy finished up his NFL season with great dignity and class, and didn't talk about anything until his contract was over with San Francisco. The way my former teammate and acting athletic director, Jim Hackett, handled that whole process and there were so many factors that had to come together. I just kept my fingers crossed and said my prayers that this would work out.

"I'm just grateful that I've had the opportunity to watch Jimmy and his family come back here and be such a big part of the Michigan family again."

Jamie Morris, who left Michigan in 1987 as the school's career and single-season rushing leader, played all but one of his seasons with Harbaugh. What did he see in his quarterback that hinted he would be coaching some day?

"The way he was in the huddle," said Morris. "He knew what every person had to do, and he would tell you what to do.

"But, most importantly, he was a leader of men."

Jerry Hanlon, his position coach at Michigan, recalled how Harbaugh's development as a quarterback tied into the coach he became:

"When I coached the quarterbacks," said Hanlon, "we did a lot of different things from what other quarterbacks coaches did. Our quarterbacks not only had to know the basic techniques of how to play the position, they also had to learn a lot more from the standpoint of: 'OK, what's the front? What's the secondary doing? On the snap of the ball, are they doing what they're supposed to do?'

"We'd look to see if they were in zone or man-to-man [coverage]. It could look like zone on the snap and turn to man, and vice versa. We had to learn how to block them and what was the strong side and what was the weak side of the play, so you knew where to go. And we had to read on the move so you knew what you wanted to do with the football, particularly in the passing game. So we would go in the room with an old projector and discuss what happened on plays. And Jimmy was as good of a student as I ever had in trying to learn all those things. He really studied it and studied the game of football.

"We did an awful lot of play-calling at the line of scrimmage. We very seldom ever called a play in the huddle. We gave them options on what to call, but they had to really be tuned-in to what we were trying to do to allow a quarterback to have that much leeway. And Jimmy Harbaugh was one that I had that I felt could go out there and be like another coach on the field. He had to be an extension of you to get the things done that you wanted to do. Jimmy Harbaugh was a kid I felt pretty confident in when I threw him out into the fray. He was going to do what he was taught to do, and it's carried over into his pro career. I had a couple of his former coaches in the pros come in here and talk to me about what we did to get him that way. And so, I think it's just carried over into his coaching career."

Dan Dierdorf, an All-American tackle at Michigan in 1970, observed Harbaugh as the San Francisco coach while doing national TV broadcasts and began doing analysis for Michigan's radio network in 2014. He's attended many team practices since then.

"Jim has a personality that is endearing to the players," said Dierdorf. "I doubt it's because he's tried to pattern himself after Bo, but Jim's very demanding. The

Michigan players practice long and hard, and they'd practice longer if the rules allowed. He has the ability to push these guys, but he's got enough of a personality that they love playing for him and respond to it.

"It's a real balancing act for a coach to have the right mixture of pushing, prodding, and yelling and at the same time have the ability to be their friend, so they know they can come and talk to you about anything. Jim has got that balance."

Dierdorf said Harbaugh also has the trust of his players because "he never throws them under the bus.

"And if you don't think the players are keeping score on whether their coach has their back," said Dierdorf, "then you don't know anything about sports. Every player on the Michigan team knows Jim Harbaugh will never violate that trust no matter how crappy they play or how tempting it is to do it.

"All we have to do now is win."

Hanlon chuckled and added, "He's got to get better, like we all do."

Michigan had a five-game improvement in Harbaugh's first season, going 10–3 in 2015 and winning a 41–7 blowout over Florida in the Buffalo Wild Wings Citrus Bowl. Harbaugh groomed Jake Rudock into a future NFL quarterback to spark the offense, and defensive coordinator D. J. Durkin drew raves on that side of the ball and became the head coach at Maryland.

The Wolverines followed that up with another 10-win season, and adding Don Brown as the defensive coordinator ended up being a surprising upgrade as the defense led the nation in total defense, passing yards allowed, and third-down defense. Michigan was ranked No. 3 when it lost a 30–27 double-overtime game at No. 2 Ohio State and was one play away from reaching the College Football Playoff. The Wolverines also had a Heisman Trophy finalist in defensive standout Jabrill Peppers.

So the program's ascension continued.

The 8–5 record in 2017 wasn't what was expected. But Harbaugh had to replace seventeen starters (eleven were NFL draft picks), and injuries forced him to use three quarterbacks with original starter Wilton Speight, John O'Korn, and Brandon Peters. The offense was inconsistent. Still, the defense remained stout, finishing third in total defense, and once again finishing No. 1 in passing yards allowed and third-down defense.

Harbaugh had all but five starters returning in 2018 with standout defensive linemen Rashan Gary and Chase Winovich, second team All-America linebacker Devin Bush, playmaking viper Khaleke Hudson, lock-down cornerbacks David Long and Lavert Hill, tough offensive guard Ben Bredeson, playmaking tailbacks

Karan Higdon and Chris Evans, long-range field goal kicker Quinn Nordin, and rising star tight ends Zach Gentry and Sean McKeon.

Starting safeties Tyree Kinnel and Josh Metellus returned, and so did a pair of young guards, Cesar Ruiz and Michael Onwenu, who got some starts and showed plenty of promise. Ruiz also plays center.

Three freshmen wide receivers—Donovan Peoples-Jones, Tarik Black, and Nico Collins—all showed they're capable of making an impact.

Freshman fullback Ben Mason, who impressed veteran players with his weight room dedication and toughness, is definitely one to watch. So is quarterback Dylan McCaffrey, who drew raves from defensive coordinator Brown as the demonstration team leader while redshirting as a freshman. Defensive tackle Aubrey Solomon, who earned starts as a true freshman, should be the next big thing on the D-line. Freshman safety J'Marick Woods is a heavy hitter with loads of promise.

Shea Patterson, a five-star recruit whom many considered the nation's top prep quarterback in 2016, transferred from Ole Miss to Michigan.

"I envision continued success," said Jim Brandstatter, the Wolverines' radio network play-by-play man who was an offensive tackle on Schembechler's first teams. "With Jim, one, he's proven to be a darned good recruiter and we know he can coach. We've seen that. He's done a great job with his staff, and I don't know if he gets enough credit for the guys like Don Brown, and these position coaches that are now spreading their wings out to different places. And the kids are getting really well-coached, and they're very talented kids. So I see nothing but great success ahead.

"I've always said to win a national title you've got to be really good, you've got to be injury free, and you've got to be lucky. Your schedule has to work out or the other team that's really great on your schedule might lose their quarterback three weeks before you play them and you get a little bit of a break. All of those things kind of play into the factors for a national title. But Michigan, I think, will be great, will be on the scene, and will be in the mix for a Final Four berth as long as Jim Harbaugh is here and continues to recruit and do the things that he's been doing."

# Acknowledgments

We would like to thank those who took the time to talk with us about Michigan football: Jerry Green, Jim Brandstatter, Mike Lantry, Dan Dierdorf, Jerry Hanlon, Reggie McKenzie, Steve Everitt, Jon Jansen, Jack Miller, Mason Cole, Shemy Schembechler, Fritz Seyferth, Rick Leach, John Wangler, Jim Harbaugh, Jamie Morris, Desmond Howard, Tyrone Wheatley, Lloyd Carr, Charles Woodson, Brian Griese, Glen Steele, Tai Streets, Sam Sword, Eric Mayes, Tom Brady, Derek Jeter, Braylon Edwards, and Greg Harden.

We greatly appreciate the helpful efforts of Greg Kinney, Brian Williams, Bruce Madej, Dave Ablauf, Chad Shepard, and Jon Falk. Also, a special thanks to those at MGoBlue.com, the University of Michigan athletic department web site, which allows us special access to all things maize and blue.

And, from the bottom of our hearts, a round of applause for those who have read our stories at various publications, websites, and blogs over the years. You have allowed us to write stories for a living, and for that we are forever grateful.

# Sources

Quotes from stories that Steve Kornacki authored as a writer for three publications were used in the following chapters:

*Ann Arbor News*: Coach Bo Schembechler; Jim Harbaugh Begins a Quarterback Tradition.

*Detroit Free Press*: 1969: A Monumental Upset of No. 1 Ohio State; Desmond Howard, 1991 Heisman Trophy Winner; and Biakabutuka Runs Wild Past Buckeyes.

MGoBlue.com: Rob Lytle, Tailback Extraordinaire; Tyrone Wheatley's Rose Bowl Romp; Desmond Howard, 1991 Heisman Trophy Winner; Tom Brady: Learning to Believe in Himself; Braylon Edwards, Record-Breaking Receiver; and Coach Jim Harbaugh

# About the Authors

Derek Kornacki has covered the Jim Harbaugh-led Wolverines as a blogger and was a freelance writer for the *Tampa Tribune*. He studied film direction and screenplay writing at Columbia College, an art school in Chicago. Derek has a daughter, Scarlett, and enjoys music, film, and cycling. He was taught to "shake a man's hand" by Bo Schembechler.

Steve Kornacki is a national award-winning writer and editor who has worked for the *Detroit Free Press*, *Tampa Tribune*, *Orlando Sentinel*, *Ann Arbor News*, and *Fox Sports Detroit*. The first Michigan football team he covered as a beat writer was coached by Bo Schembechler and had a freshman quarterback named Jim Harbaugh. Steve is the author of *Go Blue! Michigan's Greatest Football Stories*. He lives in Plymouth, Michigan, and writes features and columns for the University of Michigan at MGoBlue.com.